GENRE

Genre is a key means by which we categorise the many forms of literature and culture. However, it is also much more than that: in talk and writing, in music and images, in film and television, genres actively generate and shape our knowledge of the world. Understanding genre as a dynamic process rather than a set of stable rules, this book explores:

- the relation of simple to complex genres
- the history of literary genre in theory
- the generic organisation of implied meanings
- the structuring of interpretation by genre
- the uses of genre in teaching

John Frow's lucid exploration of this fascinating concept will be essential reading for students of literary and cultural studies.

John Frow is Professor of English at the University of Melbourne.

THE NEW CRITICAL IDIOM

SERIES EDITOR: JOHN DRAKAKIS, UNIVERSITY OF STIRLING

The New Critical Idiom is an invaluable series of introductory guides to today's critical terminology. Each book:

- provides a handy, explanatory guide to the use (and abuse) of the term
- offers an original and distinctive overview by a leading literary and cultural critic
- relates the term to the larger field of cultural representation.

With a strong emphasis on clarity, lively debate and the widest possible breadth of examples, *The New Critical Idiom* is an indispensable approach to key topics in literary studies.

Also available in this series:

The Author by Andrew Bennett

Autobiography by Linda Anderson

Adaptation and Appropriation by Julie Sanders

Class by Gary Day

Colonialism/Postcolonialism Second edition by Ania Loomba

Comedy by Andrew Stott

Crime Fiction by John Scaggs

Culture/Metaculture by Francis Mulhern

Difference by Mark Currie

Discourse by Sara Mills

Drama/Theatre/Performance by Simon Shepherd and Mick Wallis

Dramatic Monologue by Glennis Byron

Ecocriticism by Greg Garrard

Genders by David Glover and Cora Kaplan

Genre by John Frow

Gothic by Fred Botting

Historicism by Paul Hamilton

Humanism by Tony Davies

Ideology by David Hawkes

Interdisciplinarity by Joe Moran

Intertextuality by Graham Allen

Irony by Claire Colebrook

Literature by Peter Widdowson

Magic(al) Realism by Maggie Ann Bowers

Metre, Rhythm and Verse Form by Philip Hobsbaum

Modernism by Peter Childs

Myth by Laurence Coupe

Narrative by Paul Cobley

Parody by Simon Dentith

Pastoral by Terry Gifford

The Postmodern by Simon Malpas

Realism by Pam Morris

Romance by Barbara Fuchs

Romanticism by Aidan Day

Science Fiction by Adam Roberts

Sexuality by Joseph Bristow

Stylistics by Richard Bradford

Subjectivity by Donald E. Hall

The Sublime by Philip Shaw

The Unconscious by Antony Easthope

GENRE

John Frow

Routledge
Taylor & Francis Group

LONDON AND NEW YORK

First published 2006
by Routledge
2 Park Square, Milton Park, Abingdon, Oxon OX14 4RN

Simultaneously published in the USA and Canada
by Routledge
270 Madison Ave, New York, NY 10016

Routledge is an imprint of the Taylor & Francis Group

© 2005 John Frow

Typeset in Garamond and Scala Sans by
Taylor & Francis Books
Printed and bound in Great Britain by
TJ International Ltd, Padstow, Cornwall

British Library Cataloguing in Publication Data
A catalogue record for this book is available from the British Library

Library of Congress Cataloging-in-Publication Data
A catalog record for this book has been requested

ISBN 0–415–28062–1 (hbk)
ISBN 0–415–28063–X (pbk)

Taylor & Francis Group is the Academic Division of T&F Informa plc.

CONTENTS

SERIES EDITOR'S PREFACE   vii
ACKNOWLEDGEMENTS   viii

Introduction   1

1   **Approaching genre**   6
    Preliminary questions   6
    The situation of genre   12
    The performance of genre   17

2   **Simple and complex genres**   29
    Simple forms: the riddle   29
    Generic complexity   40
    Citation and intertextuality   45

3   **Literary genre theory**   51
    Genre as taxonomy   51
    Presentational modes: Plato and Aristotle   55
    The natural forms   58
    Genres and modes   63
    Poetics and history   68

4   **Implication and relevance**   72
    The structural dimensions of genre   72
    Implication and presupposition   77
    Genre as schema   83
    Generic truths: Philosophy   87
    Generic truths: History   92

5 Genre and interpretation   **100**
     Reading genre   100
     The frame   103
     Generic cues   109
     Figures of genre   114

6 System and history   **124**
     Genre systems   124
     Synchrony and diachrony   128
     Genrification   137
     Teaching genre   139

GLOSSARY   145
BIBLIOGRAPHY   156
INDEX   166

SERIES EDITOR'S PREFACE

The New Critical Idiom is a series of introductory books which seeks to extend the lexicon of literary terms, in order to address the radical changes which have taken place in the study of literature during the last decades of the twentieth century. The aim is to provide clear, well-illustrated accounts of the full range of terminology currently in use, and to evolve histories of its changing usage.

The current state of the discipline of literary studies is one where there is considerable debate concerning basic questions of terminology. This involves, among other things, the boundaries which distinguish the literary from the non-literary; the position of literature within the larger sphere of culture; the relationship between literatures of different cultures; and questions concerning the relation of literary to other cultural forms within the context of interdisciplinary studies.

It is clear that the field of literary criticism and theory is a dynamic and heterogeneous one. The present need is for individual volumes on terms which combine clarity of exposition with an adventurousness of perspective and a breadth of application. Each volume will contain as part of its apparatus some indication of the direction in which the definition of particular terms is likely to move, as well as expanding the disciplinary boundaries within which some of these terms have been traditionally contained. This will involve some re-situation of terms within the larger field of cultural representation, and will introduce examples from the area of film and the modern media in addition to examples from a variety of literary texts.

Acknowledgements

I am deeply grateful to Alastair Fowler, David Duff, and Dana Polan for their generosity in reading and commenting on the manuscript. Liz Thompson reminded me that the reader's eyes will see in ways other than mine do; John Drakakis did a masterly job of reducing the proliferating parentheses in the text he saw, and of bringing a greater 'clarity of exposition' to it. Sandra helped bring a much greater clarity to my life, and the book is dedicated to her.

The quotations from Rosmarie Waldrop's translations of Jacques Roubaud's *The Plurality of Worlds of Lewis* are used by kind permission of the Dalkey Archive Press.

INTRODUCTION

This book is about the kinds or genres of speech, writing, images, and organised sound: forms of talk and writing, of drawing and painting and sculpting, of architecture, of music, and mixed forms like film, television, opera, and drama. It is a book about how genres organise verbal and non-verbal discourse, together with the actions that accompany them, and how they contribute to the social structuring of meaning.

I take it that all texts are strongly shaped by their relation to one or more genres, which in turn they may modify. In certain areas of criticism it is assumed that genre is a term that applies to some texts and not to others: thus we speak of genre films, meaning strongly defined genres such as the Western or the heist movie; of genre painting, meaning a style of representation of everyday scenes, defined by opposition to paintings on larger historical themes; and of genre fiction, meaning for the most part such popular genres as the detective story or science fiction. Genre in this sense indicates the formulaic and the conventional. Now, it is certainly the case that this usage points to real distinctions between different textual functions, different audience structures, and different patterns of reading. But for the purposes of this book I treat this way of speaking about genre as irrelevant because it obscures the extent to which even the most complex and least formulaic of texts is shaped and organised by its relation to generic structures. Genre, as I use the term here, is a universal dimension of textuality.

In what follows, I am not concerned with the question of *how* to classify or to recognise genres, and the book is neither a description nor an endorsement of existing classifications. It is not designed to be comprehensive, to 'cover' the range of genres, because I assume that there is no master list. Rather than developing a detailed description of all the genres that there are, what I do is try to think about the uses of genre: how do genres work in practice, what do we do with genre classifications, what are their social dimensions? In particular, the book is about how genres actively generate and shape knowledge of the world; and about how generically shaped knowledges are bound up with the exercise of power, where power is understood as being exercised in discourse, as well as elsewhere, but is never simply external to discourse. In that sense I understand genre as a form of symbolic action: the generic organisation of language, images, gestures, and sound makes things happen by actively shaping the way we understand the world.

The book's central argument, then, is that far from being merely 'stylistic' devices, genres create effects of reality and truth, authority and plausibility, which are central to the different ways the world is understood in the writing of history or of philosophy or of science, or in painting, or in everyday talk. These effects are not, however, fixed and stable, since texts – even the simplest and most formulaic – do not 'belong' to genres but are, rather, uses of them; they refer not to 'a' genre but to a field or economy of genres, and their complexity derives from the complexity of that relation. Uses of texts ('readings') similarly refer, and similarly construct a position in relation to that economy.

I'm not unaware, of course, that this book itself has a generic shape, that of the 'introductory guide' which is lucidly described in the Series Editor's Preface. You will judge for yourself whether I manage to 'combine clarity of exposition with an adventurousness of perspective and a breadth of application'; more importantly, I hope that by the end of the book you will recognise the kind of speaking position that is constructed for me and for you by this genre, and the kinds of effect of knowledge and truth it generates. Needless to say, I hope that you will be able to see a little further through them.

The shape of the book is as follows. In the first chapter, 'Approaching Genre', I set out what I take to be some of the basic problems in think-ing about genre – questions about how genres incorporate and invoke structures of knowledge, about the kinds of classification they perform, about historical continuity and difference, and about the kinds of action they perform upon the world. I think about the material embedding of genre structures in bookshop shelves and filing systems and television guides and everyday talk, and about their organising force in everyday life. I think about how genres relate to recurrent situations. And I try to stress that genres are not fixed and pre-given forms by thinking about texts as performances of genre rather than reproductions of a class to which they belong, and by following Derrida in stressing the impor-tance of edges and margins – that is, in stressing the open-endedness of generic frames.

In Chapter 2, 'Simple and Complex Genres', I take up from Bakhtin and Jolles the concept of certain 'simple forms' of textuality that they take to be the building blocks of more complex forms, and I explore the genre of the riddle to see how well the concept works. I find that, although it is in some ways useful, it can't really be sustained because even the most apparently basic forms produce complex effects. In the process, however, I hope to say some interesting things about how rid-dles work and, more generally, about how genres are structured. What this exploration opens up for me is an investigation of relations *between* genres, something that I take to be a central feature of how they func-tion; I look at reported speech as an example of one such relationship, and then more generally at citation and other forms of intertextuality which I believe illuminate the core processes of textuality.

Chapter 3, 'Literary Genre Theory', begins by meditating upon the classificatory functions of genre and placing them in the context of human classification in general. I look briefly at biological models of taxonomy and at some of the metaphors through which genre has been understood – the family, the species, the contract, the speech act, and so on. Most of the chapter is taken up with a historical account of genre theory, from the poetics of Plato and Aristotle through the Romantic notion of a small set of 'natural forms', to a number of con-temporary accounts that seek to deal with the diversity and historicity of genres. I follow Fowler and others in distinguishing genres from modes, and I finish the chapter by seeking to bring together the different logics involved in thinking about genre in terms of a poetics (a systematic account of structures) and in terms of historical description of the genres that have actually existed.

Chapter 4, 'Implication and Relevance', extends some of my provisional conclusions by mapping out the three overlapping and intersecting dimensions along which I think genre is organised and by which particular genres produce their effects of truth and authority: the dimensions of formal organisation, of rhetorical structure, and of thematic content (roughly: how genres are shaped, the speaking positions they enable, and what they are typically about). I then move to think about how these structures project generically specific 'worlds': more or less coherent structures of meaning built up out of presupposed knowledges which genres at once invoke and reinforce. I use (in a somewhat critical manner) certain theories from natural language philosophy and cognitive psychology to talk about the processing of information, and I argue that genre is central to the social organisation of knowledge. In the rest of this chapter I look, briefly and schematically, at how the various genres of philosophy and of history organise disciplinary knowledges in specific and distinctive ways.

Chapter 5, 'Genre and Interpretation', explores the idea that genre is a set of cues guiding our reading of texts. Here the notion of the frame becomes important: I use it to talk about how we recognise differences in genre, and about the contextual nature of cues. This chapter moves through a number of textual examples to examine the play between a structured text and a process of reading that responds to the text's strategic intentions, but which may, of course, productively ignore them. Genre is one of the ways in which texts seek to control the uncertainty of communication, and it may do so by building in figures of itself, models of how it should be read. The complexity of genre means, however, that these models can never be taken as straightforward guidelines, and indeed that notions of a one-way flow between genre and text can never be particularly useful.

In Chapter 6, 'System and History', finally, I take up the idea that genres exist only in relation to other genres, and that these relations are more or less systemically ordered at any point in time. Genres belong to an economy: a set of interdependent positions that organise the universe of knowledge and value. Yet the content of such systems and of particular genres within them is constantly changing. I look at the history of the poetic form called the elegy in order to demonstrate how such changes are worked out in different historical circumstances as the relations between this poetic form and others mutate; and, using Hollywood movies as my example, I think some more about the institutional underpinnings by which genres come into being and are given authority and weight. I finish the book by turning these questions about genre back to the classroom in which genre forms are so crucially transmitted, and where we learn to think with and through them as we learn our culture.

1

APPROACHING GENRE

PRELIMINARY QUESTIONS

Consider the following piece of writing, displayed recently for a few hours on hoardings in the streets of Edinburgh:

RAPE CASE
JUDGE IN
NEW STORM

This very transient and very simple **text**, referring to a judge deemed to be handing down lenient sentences, works with a number of 'deep' suppositions. It supposes a reader walking or driving in the street whose attention needs to be caught by large and bold lettering, and who knows that these words are on display because they are tied to a story in the newspaper whose name is inscribed on the border of the poster. It assumes that the reader believes the story it tells is factually true, and that it is newsworthy, not trivial (this is one reason why the word 'storm' here cannot be read literally: judges caught in the rain are not news). And it supposes that the reader possesses the **information** necessary to understand what this 'case' was, and hence what the *old* 'storm' was in which this judge was involved. (The reader must also know enough about legal process to know what a judge and a case are.)

Most of the knowledge required to read and understand this text is knowledge about the *kind* of writing it is: knowledge about its genre. Some of the knowledge required of the reader looks like knowledge about the real world rather than knowledge about texts and genres; but the 'rape case' with which the reader is deemed to be familiar is defined by the fact that it was extensively written about in previous issues of the newspaper; the 'storms', both old and new, are storms in a newspaper, and the knowledge the reader is expected to have is **intertextual**: knowledge of earlier reports and earlier controversies.

This piece of writing establishes a set of **knowledges**, then, by invoking them in a compressed form; like all texts, this one is elliptical, setting out new information on the basis of old information which is not explicitly given but which it supposes its reader to have. (It may be that the reader does not have it, of course: they may not be able to read, they may be a child, or they may just not have heard about the previous story: they may not belong, that is to say, to the **discourse community** which is invoked and renewed by this hoarding.) In its small way, this text constructs a **world** which is generically specific. It is different in kind from the worlds performed in other genres of writing, although it will overlap with some of them.

In calling this story a 'world' I don't mean to imply that it is a *complete* world, the infinitely complex totality of everything that exists. This is a schematic world, a limited piece of reality, which is sketched in outline and carved out from a larger continuum. It has its own coordinates of space and time: a strip of time stretching from the 'old' to the 'new' 'storm', and the geographical and cultural space of Scotland. This world is populated by specific players (judges, criminals, victims, and ordinary people) and infused with a moral ethos which brings with it certain attitudes to these players (judges are potentially out of touch with reality and so tend to be overly lenient in their sentencing, criminals should be punished in accordance with their crimes, ordinary people have a stake in these issues because they are always potential victims).

The definition of space, time, moral ethos, and players is an effect of the genre which is actualised as story in the hoarding headlines and more fully articulated in the successively more expansive pieces of text (heading, sub-heading, first paragraph, subsequent paragraphs) in the newspaper itself. In addition to this **thematic** content, the headline is characterised by a number of distinctive **formal features** which set it apart as a genre: compression, nominalisation or suppression of verb forms, the use of large and bold type, and a specialised vocabulary in which 'storm', for example, means 'furious controversy'. In another, even more strikingly nominalised headline from a few days earlier – **DEATH MUM TRAGEDY PROBE CALL** – the word 'probe' takes on a meaning ('enquiry' or 'investigation') that it possesses in few if any other contexts, and the syntax twists itself into a chain of implicit causal linkages which requires a quite specialised knowledge of the genre if it is to be translated into an expanded form ('there have been calls for an official investigation into the circumstances surrounding the tragic death of a mother of small children'). Note finally that, although the two texts belong to one of the simplest of genres, they nevertheless manage between them to refer, in the course of eleven words, to five other literary and non-literary genres: the legal *case*, the *'storm'* (controversy), *tragedy*, the *'probe'* (official enquiry), and the *'call'*. These texts are at once generically structured and **metageneric** in their reference: they refer from one genre to another.

Suppose, though, that I modified the words of the headline to produce a slightly different text – something like:

SCAPEGRACE
RAPE CASE
JUDGE IN
NEW STORM

and that these words appeared not on a street hoarding but in an anthology of poetry. Framed and lineated in this way, they would be read as a poem (of sorts), and we would attend to the sound of its words and the rhythm of its enjambed lines in a way that we didn't with the first text, where the lineation, the spondaic rhythms, the nearly equal letter count in each line (8–7–8), and the internal assonance (*ra*pe *ca*se) were disattended, treated as inconsequential. Certain formal features become salient in the new text which would have been disregarded in the hoarding: a dancing rhythm, for example, which generates a certain playfulness in the place of moral indignation.

Yet it is not the formal features in themselves that lead us to make a different generic assignment, although it helps that I have manipulated the text to call attention to them. It is, rather, the different *framing* of the two texts – their placing in different contexts – that governs the different salience of their formal features, and of all the other dimensions of genre that are entailed in this shift of **frame**: a different **structure of address**, a different moral universe, and different truth-effects. Or rather, there is an interplay between the cues given by formal features, such as assonance and rhythm, and the reframing that reinforces their role; and these intertwined effects of **form** and framing give rise to new patterns of meaning and tone.

Let me summarise the different structural dimensions that have emerged from my discussion of the genre of the headline to this point. In brief, they look like this:

- a set of *formal features*: the visual structure of the type size and its relation to the page; the organisation of sounds, much more strongly foregrounded when the text is rewritten as a 'poem'; a syntactic structure which works above all through nominalisation of verb phrases; and a vocabulary which is, in part, specific to the genre of the headline
- a *thematic structure* which draws upon a set of highly conventional **topics** or *topoi* (the lenient judge, the tragically dead mum) and projects a schematic but coherent and plausible world from these materials
- a *situation of address* in which an anonymous speaker addresses a random and undifferentiated reader passing by in the street. This **speaking position** brings with it a certain kind of authority and moral force ('what I say is true, and I know that you share my moral concern'), or what I earlier called 'tone'
- a more general *structure of **implication***, which both invokes and presupposes a range of relevant background knowledges, and in so doing sets up a certain complicity with the reader
- a *rhetorical function*: the text is structured in such a way as to achieve certain pragmatic effects: to catch the attention of a distracted reader with sufficient force to persuade them to buy a copy of the newspaper; to reinforce a set of populist moral judgements
- Finally, the generic structure of this text is established, and many of these other dimensions activated, by a physical *setting* which takes

on the force of a regulative *frame*. This frame differentiates the genre of this text from other possible genres, alerts us to the way it works (its rhetorical function), and draws our attention towards some of its features and away from others.

Genre, we might say, is a set of conventional and highly organised constraints on the production and interpretation of meaning. In using the word 'constraint' I don't mean to say that genre is simply a restriction. Rather, its structuring effects are productive of meaning; they shape and guide, in the way that a builder's form gives shape to a pour of concrete, or a sculptor's mould shapes and gives structure to its materials. Generic structure both enables and restricts meaning, and is a basic condition for meaning to take place. I take it that genre theory is, or should be, about the ways in which different structures of meaning and truth are produced in and by the various kinds of writing, talking, painting, filming, and acting by which the universe of **discourse** is structured. That is why genre matters: it is central to human meaning-making and to the social struggle over meanings. No speaking or writing or any other symbolically organised action takes place other than through the shapings of generic codes, where 'shaping' means both 'shaping by' and 'shaping of': acts and structures work upon and modify each other.

At the same time, there are real and perhaps intractable conceptual difficulties involved in thinking about genre. Assuming that we want to do something other than simply list the genres that there are (a list which is potentially endless, not least because new genres are constantly emerging and old ones changing their function), we would have to think about some of the following questions:

- How do we know what knowledge is built into the structure of a genre? 'Built into' in what sense? How are these background knowledges organised, and what determines their relevance to the interpretation of a text?
- How is a text assigned to a particular genre? What operations must readers (listeners, viewers ...) perform in order to generalise from a specific piece of text to the **class** of which it is a member?
- Are there in fact such well-defined classes, or are the genres of talk or writing or painting (and so on) looser, fuzzier, more open-ended

than, say, a mathematical set or a biological species? What model of generality best captures the way genres operate?

- What guarantees that we correctly recognise this class? Is there such a thing as 'correct' genre assignment, or is the process of generalisation looser and more variable? When the form or the function of a genre changes, is it still the 'same' genre?

- Conversely, what relations hold between all the members of a class? How many features must they have in common before they count as 'belonging' to it? How do we know which features are relevant to a judgement about genre? And is the point of thinking about genre to assign texts to the relevant class, or rather to say something useful about the meaning or the working of a text?

- Do texts in fact 'belong' to a genre, in a simple type/token relation (general form/particular instance), or should we posit some more complex relation, in which texts would 'perform' a genre, or modify it in 'using' it, or only partially realise a generic form, or would be composed of a mix of different genres?

- What happens when genre frames change, as in the case when a newspaper hoarding is read as a poem, and when the 'same' text is reinscribed in a book as an 'example' of a genre? Do texts have a determinate structure, and if they do, to what extent does this limit the ways they can be read?

- To what extent and in what way does the setting or frame of a text govern the salience and function of its various elements? If we know the genre to which a text belongs, can we predict what it will be like?

- What exactly is the 'setting' of a genre? Is it a matter of physical context, or of something immaterial? Where does its regulative force come from? Is it an empirical fact, or does its power derive from the fact that it is a *kind* of setting?

- Given the diversity of dimensions along which genre can be defined (formal structure, thematic structure, mode of presentation, rhetorical function …), is it possible to produce a coherent account of the interrelations between them?

This book does not aim to solve the many problems of **taxonomy**, to produce an overall 'theory' of genre, or to elaborate a systematic account of the relations between texts and genres. But I do assume that these are interesting problems, because they go to the heart of the way meaning and truth are structured, circulated, and controlled in a set of complex social relations of discourse. The category of genre is a privileged object of study because it supposes that questions of meaning and truth are always questions of form and of the situation of utterance (these are questions I explore more fully later in this chapter); because it has to do at once with **systems** and with historical change; and because it ranges over every level of the symbolic order, of our social world and of every other.

THE SITUATION OF GENRE

Reflection on genres and the distinctions between them is built deep into ordinary talk and writing and into systems for the ordering of texts and talk. We have already seen it happening, spontaneously and without conscious intent, in the two newspaper headlines. It may take the form of explicit guidelines, or of informal reflection by way of 'rules, silences, gestures, ... complaints' (Giltrow 2002: 202): small hints that warn of boundaries. It is embedded in filing systems, in the organisation of books and journals in libraries, in school syllabuses, in the instructions for filling out tax returns, in Powerpoint templates, and in online discussions of list etiquette. It flourishes 'at the thresholds of communities of discourse, patrolling or controlling individuals' participation in the collective, foreseeing or suspecting their involvements elsewhere, differentiating, initiating, restricting, inducing forms of activity, rationalising and representing the relations of the genre to the community that uses it' (Giltrow 2002: 203). Embodied in sorting mechanisms that are continuously reinforced by discussion, by use, even by contestation, generic classification is at once 'conceptual (in the sense of persistent patterns of change and action, resources for organising abstractions) and material (in the sense of being inscribed, transported, and affixed to stuff)' (Bowker and Star 1999: 289). This is to say that genre is not just a matter of codes and conventions, but that it also calls into play systems of use, durable social institutions, and the organisation of physical space.

At another level, classification is an industrial matter. It is enacted in publishers' catalogues and booksellers' classifications, in the allocation

of time-slots for television shows and in television guides, in the guidelines and deliberations of arts organisations, and in the discourses of
marketing and publicity, together with the whole apparatus of review-
ing and listing and recommending, that drive so much of film production. The consumers of books, recorded music, television and film are
ongoingly schooled, and actively school themselves, in the fine-grained
details of genre. But this 'schooling' translates into difficult and precari-
ous judgements: is this story I'm hearing meant to be serious or joking?
Do I read this movie as melodrama or pastiche? Readers and viewers and
listeners have constant resort to a kind of folk classification, an unsys-
tematically systematic taxonomy which feels intuitive and yet covers
most of the difficult and ambiguous cases they are likely to encounter,
and translates an experience of texts into the terms of a naturalised moral
order ('I don't like Hollywood action movies because they're so violent').

'Folk classification' is perhaps a patronising way of putting it.
Almost all classification systems have a kind of 'folk' logic to them, in the
sense that George Lakoff speaks of there being a folk theory of categorisation itself, which says 'that things come in well-defined kinds, that the
kinds are characterised by shared properties, and that there is one right
taxonomy of the kinds' (Lakoff 1987: 21, cited in Bowker and Star
1999: 33). It's easy enough to see arbitrariness and incoherence in the
organisation of shelves in the video store or the record shop: are the categories of 'comedy', 'drama', 'war', 'action', 'adult', 'science fiction' in the
one place and 'rock', 'easy listening', 'soundtracks', 'pop', and 'world music'
in the other meant to be mutually exclusive, or do they overlap? Yet, as we
shall see in Chapter 3, just the same lack of internal coherence characterises
almost all attempts at a systematic scholarly analysis of the literary genres, which uneasily mix thematic, formal, modal, and functional criteria.

In one important sense, however, these shortcomings and inconsistencies
are irrelevant. Genre classifications are real. They have an organising
force in everyday life. They are embedded in material infrastructures and
in the recurrent practices of classifying and differentiating kinds of
symbolic action. And they bind abstruse and delicate negotiations
of meaning to the social situations in which they occur. It would almost
be a definition of genre to say that it is a *relationship* between textual
structures and the **situations** that occasion them, although, as we shall
see, the concept of 'situation' needs to be defined with some care.

This emphasis on the social and situational underpinnings of genre corresponds closely to the way much recent work in the field of rhetoric has tended to think about it: as a structured complex which has a strategic character and interacts with the demands of an environment. For Campbell and Jamieson, 'a genre is composed of a constellation of recognisable forms bound together by an internal dynamic', and this dynamic is a 'fusion of substantive, stylistic, and situational elements' which works as a range of potential 'strategic responses to the demands of the situation' (Campbell and Jamieson 1978: 146). Genres are to be defined not in terms of the intrinsic structure of their discourse but by the *actions* they are used to accomplish; in Carolyn Miller's words, they are 'typified rhetorical actions based in recurrent situations' (Miller 1994a: 31).

The work of genre, then, is to mediate between a social situation and the text which realises certain features of this situation, or which responds strategically to its demands. Genre shapes strategies for occasions; it gets a certain kind of work done. But we need to make some distinctions here between the level of structure and the level of the textual event. Genre is not itself an action or a performance: it is a 'typified' action, a structural kind. Similarly, the situation to which it is adapted is not a one-off event but a recurrent form. The recurrence that underlies genre patterns 'is not a material situation (a real, objective, factual event) but our construal of a type' (Miller 1994a: 29), and genre 'acquires meaning' from the kinds of situation it relates to (Miller 1994a: 37). It 'embodies the type of recurring situation that evokes it, and ... provides a strategic response to that situation' (Coe *et al.* 2002: 6).

A variety of metaphors operate here to try to catch something of the complexity of that relation between genre as typified action and situation as recurrent form: genre is 'based' in situation and 'acquires meaning' from it; it 'embodies' it and is 'evoked by' it, and at the same time it 'provides a strategic response' to it. The patterns of genre, that is to say, are at once shaped by a type of situation and in turn shape the rhetorical actions that are performed in response to it.

Let us see how this relation works out concretely in the case of the two different settings in which the 'rape case judge' text was placed. In the case of the headline, the setting was in the first instance a physical one: street hoardings close to a newsagent's shop or a paperseller's box. This setting is determined by the marketing strategies of the news industry, and sets material limits on the way the headlines are presented. But the actual physical detail will differ slightly from place to place; what matters is the *kind* of setting this is, the kind of information embedded in it, and how this information gives a certain constant shape to the daily-changing messages performed within this framework. We could imagine this information in the form of a set of reading instructions about the various structural dimensions of the message: the most general instruction specifies that this message belongs to the 'news' genre, and should thus be read as factual, relevant, and transient; lower-level messages specify an appropriate thematic range (the legal system, tragic deaths ...), relevant formal structures (bold type, nominalisation, compression ...), and a specific kind of rhetorical authority (the particular form of credibility imputed to tabloid newspapers). Roughly the same information could, however, be conveyed by a quite different physical setting: a similar headline could, for example, be included in a digest of current news stories sent by email to newspaper subscribers, with a link to an electronic version of the full story. The material grounding is quite different, but the generic pattern would be comparable, if not exactly the same.

In the case of the reworked version of this headline that I imagined being published in an anthology of poetry, the physical setting would activate quite different generic instructions. Here, the setting of the words on the page of a book, the ratio of print to blank paper, the convention of lineation, and the context of other texts which the title and various other cues give us to understand as '**literary**', all have the effect of redirecting our expectations of how the text will work. The most general specification of the text as a poem will invite us to read it as a fictional imitation of action rather than as a direct **representation** of a real event, and the foregrounding of formal structures (rhythm, visual layout) will direct us to give greater semantic weight to these features than they would otherwise carry.

The 'situation' to which a genre responds, and which is in some sense built into its own structure, is thus only at one level an empirical event. To the extent that it shapes and regulates the logic of genre, the situation is a recurrent or typical structure of *information*. It conveys a set of constraining instructions about the forms of rhetorical behaviour which would be appropriate to its circumstances, and thus translates a set of structural constraints into a set of generic possibilities. In the anthropologist Bronislaw Malinowski's famous phrase, it is a 'context of situation', an information-laden structure that conveys the 'purpose, aim and direction of the accompanying activities' (Malinowski 1935: 214). The linguist Michael Halliday takes up this concept as part of his argument that the 'situation type' is a *semiotic* structure, a 'constellation of meanings' made up of 'the ongoing social activity, the **role** relationships involved, and the symbolic or rhetorical channel' (Halliday 1978: 109). What Halliday calls linguistic *register*, a concept which I take to be roughly equivalent to that of genre, is then 'the configuration of semantic resources that the member of a culture typically associates with a situation type. It is the meaning potential that is accessible in a given social context' (Halliday 1978: 111), where the notion of 'meaning' refers not only to thematic content but to the complex of thematic, formal, and rhetorical dimensions.

What I am proposing is that texts respond to and are organised in accordance with two distinct but related levels of information, that of the social setting in which they occur (a setting which is a recurrent type rather than a particular time and place), and that of the genre mobilised by the setting and by contextual cues. We should not, however, assume that there is a one-to-one correspondence between setting and genre, or that genres can be read off from their setting. Some settings, such as a court of law, will make possible a number of different genres (oath-taking, deposition, cross-examination, summing up, or pronouncement of sentence, for example), and some genres, such as the complex literary forms, will be relatively indifferent to physical setting. We could use the metaphor of **translation** to think about relations between the levels of setting, genre, and text: texts translate (activate, perform, but also transform) the complex of meanings made available by the structure of the genre, which in turn translates the information structurally embedded in the situation to which it responds.

Anne Freadman develops yet another metaphor, that of the ceremony, to think about the material and situational dimensions of genre. Any performance of a text, she writes, takes place within a broader 'ceremonial' frame and involves all the constituents of the occasion: the audience, the actions of opening and concluding the performance, talk about the performance, and its demarcation from other performances. Such things as 'reading a book, attending and giving lectures, dinner conversations, filling in forms, interviews – and a host of others – are all ceremonial frames and/or the genres that occur within them' (Freadman 1988: 88). Ceremonies are like games that situate other games: 'they are the rules for the setting of a game, for constituting participants as players in that game, for placing and timing it in relation to other places and times' (Freadman 1988: 71). We can say, then, that the ceremonial 'frames a time and space, setting it apart from others, and marking its specificity' (Freadman 1988: 88).

Again, this has the effect of placing texts and genres in relation to social actions in a social setting. They are not, however, reducible to this setting: **textuality** is never simply a function of its situation, and the concepts of 'genre' and 'ceremonial' may or may not be coextensive, since a text may have different modes of realisation, and may take place in quite different ceremonials. Crucially, 'some genres ... subsist in different ceremonials from the ones in which they conventionally arose. In such cases, they take with them the signs of the lost ceremony, connoting that ceremony and the social relations it governs' (Freadman 1988: 89). A fragment of a home movie may be shown within a documentary, and will carry with it some of the force of its initial function. I will introduce a distinction in the next chapter between genres, such as those of everyday talk, which seem to be firmly grounded in the ceremonies of face-to-face conversation, and those, such as the more complex aesthetic genres, which are highly stylised and are governed by apparently much more abstract institutional frames; but this distinction between simple and complex genres is inherently unstable, since even the simplest of genres (and the many genres of everyday talk are by no means simple) has the capacity to cite other genres, or to parody them, or to incorporate them, or to reflect upon its own structure. If setting and genre are metacommunicative frames in relation to texts, texts in turn are always potentially **metacommunications** about their frames.

THE PERFORMANCE OF GENRE

Discourses, writes Michel Foucault, are 'practices that systematically form the objects of which they speak' (Foucault 1989: 49). Each element of this sentence matters: discourses are *practices* in the sense that they carry out an action; they are *systematic* because they are relatively coherent in the way they work; they are *formative* of objects in the very act of speaking of them, not in the sense that they create objects out of nothing but in so far as they build a weight of meaning around the categories of the world. Discourses – by which Foucault here means something very close to what I call genres – are performative structures that shape the world in the very process of putting it into speech.

Thus the discourse of the news headline elaborates the category 'judge' within a broader moral (indeed, moralistic) discourse that selects certain features of the world as being worth attending to. This thematic focus is one dimension of the headline's message, but in the very act of making a statement about the world the text also projects an attitude towards it, an evaluative tone which is built into the structure of address. The third dimension of its reality-forming effect is carried by the rhetorical channel through which it speaks: the use of bold print on a poster conveys a sense of urgency, as though the headline were a cry in the street (as in some cultures, where newspaper sellers call out the headlines, it literally is). Through these three dimensions of the message a layered series of background knowledges and values is at once evoked, called into being, and reinforced; they include knowledge about a previous controversy, a sedimented set of criticisms of lenient sentencing by judges, and a sense that this information is urgently relevant.

In Colie's words, a system of genres offers 'a set of interpretations, of "frames" or "fixes" on the world' (Colie 1973: 8). This, I think, is a way of saying that every organisation of experience is partial and is defined by the terms of one or another genre; different genres set up 'worlds' which are specific to them, although they may overlap with others, as in the very particular world of the tabloid press, made up of scandals and celebrities. In putting it this way, I am trying to get at one of the reasons why genre theory has something important to say about how realities are constructed and maintained. For Bakhtin/Medvedev (the name refers to a text attributed to Medvedev but probably jointly written), genre is 'an aggregate of the means for seeing and conceptualising reality' (Bakhtin/Medvedev 1985: 137, cited in Hanks 2000: 143); a central implication of the concept of genre is thus that the realities in and amongst which we live are not transparently conveyed to us but are mediated by systems of representation: by talk, by writing, by acting (in all senses of the word), by images, even by sound. Whereas the 'realist' genres of philosophy or history or science, and indeed of everyday common sense, tend to assume that reality is singular and external to the forms through which we apprehend it, the notion of genre as ' "frames" or "fixes" on the world' implies the divisibility of the world and the *formative* power of these representational frames. If, however, we so readily believe that we can look through pieces of text, as through a window, to an already-constituted world outside it, this is above all because 'we learn so naturally by forms and formulae that we often entirely fail to recognise them for what they are' (Colie 1973: 5).

This is the central argument of this book: that, far from being merely 'stylistic' devices, genres create effects of reality and truth which are central to the different ways the world is understood in the writing of history or philosophy or science, or in painting, or in everyday talk. The semiotic frames within which genres are embedded implicate and specify layered **ontological domains** – implicit realities which genres form as a pre-given reference, together with the effects of authority and plausibility which are specific to the genre. Genre, like formal structures generally, works at a level of **semiosis** – that is, of meaning-making – which is deeper and more forceful than that of the explicit 'content' of a text.

Let me illustrate this with two examples. The first is a reading by the literary critic Northrop Frye of Milton's 'Lycidas', a poem published in 1638 in a collective volume of elegies for a friend who had drowned and using the occasion to denounce the failings of the established church. Arguing against a familiar post-Romantic way of reading poems as acts of self-expression, Frye writes that the starting point for an informed reading of the poem must be the knowledge that it is 'an elegy in the pastoral tradition' (Frye 1963: 19). This tradition marries a set of classical and biblical sources such as Theocritus, Vergil's *Eclogues*, the 23rd Psalm, and the New Testament's imagery of Christ as shepherd, the chief link between these two strands in Milton's day being Vergil's Fourth or Messianic Eclogue, which is read as a prophecy of the birth of Christ.

The conventions of the pastoral elegy read the mourned hero not as an individual but as the dying male god of Greek mythology: Orpheus and Adonis, Shelley's Adonais, the Daphnis of Theocritus and Vergil.

He is associated with the cyclical rhythm of the seasons, and with a red or purple flower: the hyacinth, or the field poppies of the First World War. The lament for Edward King, the ostensible subject of Milton's poem, should thus not be read as a matter of personal grief or, as in some more recent criticism, of homoerotic attachment, because this is to miss the mode of 'sincerity' that Milton works with: 'Lycidas', writes Frye, 'is a passionately sincere poem because Milton was deeply interested in the structure and symbolism of funeral elegies, and had been practising since adolescence on every fresh corpse in sight, from the university beadle to the fair infant dying of a cough' (Frye 1963: 125). The 'I' that speaks in the poem is that of a professional poet in his conventional shepherd disguise, not that of the grieving personal self.

Milton is, of course, a poet who is acutely aware of the generic traditions within which he works. But just the same images and conventions emerge in the work of two other poets who seem to be resolutely hostile to conventional forms of expression. For Frye, Wordsworth's Lucy poems, a small set of lyrics published between 1798 and 1802, consist of 'flat simple statements which represent, in **literature**, the inarticulateness of personal sincerity':

> No motion has she now, no force:
> She neither hears nor sees.
>
> (Frye 1963: 125)

But this 'pretence of personal sincerity is itself a literary convention', Frye continues, and 'as soon as a death becomes a poetic image, that image is assimilated to other poetic images of death in nature, and hence Lucy inevitably becomes a figure of Proserpine [the goddess of the underworld], just as King becomes an Adonis':

> Rolled round in earth's diurnal course
> With rocks and stones and trees
>
> (Frye 1963: 125).

Something similar happens in the case of another poet who is even more strongly resistant to convention and even more strongly committed to an aesthetics of personal statement. In Walt Whitman's 'When Lilacs

Last in the Dooryard Bloomed', an elegy composed immediately after
the assassination of Abraham Lincoln in 1865:

> the dead man is not called by a pastoral name, but neither is he called
> by his historical name. He is in a coffin which is carried the length
> and breadth of the land; he is identified with a 'powerful western
> fallen star'; he is the beloved comrade of the poet, who throws
> the purple flower of the lilac on his coffin; a singing bird laments the
> death, just as the woods and caves do in 'Lycidas'. Convention, genre,
> archetype, and the autonomy of forms are all illustrated as clearly in
> Whitman as they are in Milton.
>
> (Frye 1963: 125–6)

In both cases, then, the structure of the elegiac genre imposes meanings which predominate over whatever the poet's more immediate emotions and intent might have been; and I conclude with Frye that
whatever event might have provoked the act of writing, 'the formal
inspiration, the poetic structure that crystallises around the new event,
can only be derived from other poems' (Frye 1963: 125).

My second example again sets a reading of conventions (here, those
of speech) against a notion of utterance as self-expression. Erving
Goffman's analysis of talk clearly establishes that the normal state of
affairs is dialogue, or rather the interactional structure of sequences
of responses. Yet there are certain cases, as when I laugh at my own joke
or correct something I have said, when it becomes apparent that both
the speaker's and the listener's role can be taken by a single person, indicating that these roles 'refer not to individuals as such, but to enacted
capacities' (Goffman 1981: 46). This is strikingly the case for the various genres ('forms of talk') and sub-genres he calls 'blurted vocalisation'
where there are 'more roles than persons' (Goffman 1981: 80).

One of the norms governing behaviour in public is that talking
to oneself breaches the requirement that one should be respectfully alert
in and to the social situation; like reading in public or, in more contemporary terms, wearing earphones or talking on a mobile phone, it represents a withdrawal from sociality. Failure to cease talking to oneself in
the presence of others looks like madness; and at a lower level of cen-
sure, we feel embarrassed if caught rehearsing a play in a mirror, even

though this is not strictly self-talk. Yet under certain circumstances the prohibition on talking to oneself is overridden: when one is told of the death of a loved one, for example, a certain display of emotion or concern is called for which requires a momentary withdrawal from the scene. Indeed, not to express emotion verbally ('I can't believe it!', or whatever) looks like coldness or indifference. Or again, if we try to unlock a car that turns out not to be ours, 'we are careful to blurt out a self-directed remark that properly frames our act for those who witness it', indicating to the world that we are absent-minded rather than a thief (Goffman 1981: 94). In such cases, what looks like a spontaneous expression of emotion is, Goffman argues, rather a form of scripted public display:

> Instead ... of thinking of self-talk as something blurted out under pressure, it might better be thought of as a mode of response constantly readied for those circumstances in which it is excusable. Indeed, the time and place when our private reaction is what strangers present *need* to know about is the occasion when self-talk is more than excusable.
>
> (Goffman 1981: 96–7)

Imprecations – exclamations (*shit!*) that we let out when taken by surprise – also function as:

> a form of behaviour whose very meaning is that it is something blurted out, something that has escaped control, and so such behaviour very often is, or has; but this impulsive feature does not mask the limits to which the utterance is socially processed, rather the conventionalised styling to which it is obliged to adhere.
>
> (Goffman 1981: 98)

Finally, the genre of talk that Goffman calls 'response cries' – *Oops!*, *Brr!*, *Ouch!* – tends similarly to be seen 'as a natural outflowing, a flooding up of previously contained feeling, a bursting of normal constraints, a case of being caught off guard' (Goffman 1981: 99), and similarly work, he argues, as forms of display which are strategically used for dealing with a potentially disruptive or embarrassing situation: the 'spill cry' (*Oops!*) that I make when clumsy or off-balance frames my loss of control as a momentary accident, insulating it from the rest of my behaviour and minimising the seriousness of my incompetence. These expressions are, then, the very opposite of spontaneous: they are generically structured to display spontaneity, but 'what comes to be made of a particular individual's show of "natural emotional expression" on any occasion is a considerably awesome thing not dependent on the existence anywhere of natural emotional expressions' (Goffman 1981: 108).

My argument here has of course been polemically slanted to emphasise the shaping force of generic conventions. The danger with such a slant, however, is that this shaping is understood deterministically, and genre comes to be seen as a rigid trans-historical class exercising control over the texts which it generates. Such a view is possible only if instances of speech or writing or film or painting are seen as members of previously defined classes which have causal priority over them. This, I want to argue, is at once the traditional and still prevalent view of genre, and one that mistakes the dynamic nature of all textuality.

Let me begin this further stage of my argument by drawing an elementary but crucial distinction from the anthropologist Dell Hymes. He writes:

> Genres, whether minimal or complex, are not in themselves the 'doing' of a genre, that is, are not in themselves acts, events, performances. They can occur as whole events, or in various relationships to whole events. The structure of an event may encompass preliminaries and aftermaths, may allow only for partial use of a genre, or even just allusion to it, and so forth.
>
> (Hymes 1974: 443)

A sermon is not the genre of the sermon; a Western is not the genre of the same name. A novel, or a children's story, may incorporate elements of either, without 'belonging' to either genre. The textual event is not a member of a genre-class because it may have membership in many genres, and because it is never fully defined by 'its' genre. Hymes thus continues by stressing the complexity and non-derivativeness of this relation: rather than speaking of membership in a class, he wishes 'to consider performances as *relationships to* genres, such that one can say of a performance that its materials (genres) were reported, described, run through, illustrated, quoted, enacted' (Hymes 1974: 443). Texts are acts or performances which work upon a set of generic raw materials. The relationship is one of productive elaboration rather than of derivation or determination. This is the case with all utterances, and we see it operating in literary texts whenever a writer extends the possibilities of the genre within which he or she is normally working.

In asking a question about the relation between texts and genres, and between a text and 'its' genre, traditional genre theory poses the problem as one of the relation between empirical phenomena and concepts. Postulating the text as something like a physical object, and genres as an abstract and transcendental class, it 'transforms a generic discourse into an ontological discourse' (Schaeffer 1986: 184, my translation); that is, it turns genre into something really existent, rather than a shorthand for a set of similarities and differences between texts, and it works with an absolute dichotomy between the concrete/particular and the abstract/general. The membership of a text in a genre is taken to be a relationship between a general type and a particular instance or 'token' of that type, a logical relationship that allows for no slippage, no lack of fit, between one level and the other.

Freadman describes this model as incorporating a pair of matching false assumptions about genre:

1   that a text is 'in' a genre, i.e., that it is primarily, or solely, describable in terms of the rules of one genre;

2   that genre is 'in' a text, i.e., that the features of a text will corre spond to the rules of the genre.

(Freadman 1988: 73)

Like Schaeffer, she argues that it is more useful to think of genre in terms of sets of intertextual relations – minimally, the dialogical relation of two texts in a single setting or 'ceremony' in which they 'talk' to each other, as do the 'brief' and the 'report' that follows from it; but also the relation between all those texts that are perceived to be relevantly similar to this one, as well as all those texts that are perceived to be relevantly dissimilar. A sermon is defined by its relation to other sermons, even though the kind of thing this is changes over time; but also by the fact that it is *not* a prayer or a eulogy or a political speech. To the extent that texts are understood to have a strategic or pragmatic relation to their context, genre classifications are a matter of defining the possible *uses* that texts may have. They define the potential **use values** of texts (Beebee 1994: 277), although because the range of possible uses is always open-ended, genre classifications are necessarily unstable and unpredictable. And this is so above all because texts do not simply have uses which are mapped out in advance by the genre: they are themselves *uses of genre*, performances of or allusions to the norms and conventions which form them and which they may, in turn, transform.

The conception of genre that I have been working towards here represents a shift away from an 'Aristotelian' model of taxonomy in which a relationship of hierarchical belonging between a class and its members predominates, to a more **reflexive** model in which texts are thought to use or to perform the genres by which they are shaped. Perhaps the most forceful statement of what is entailed in this shift – and a forceful putting into question of the category of genre itself – is that made by the post-structuralist philosopher Jacques Derrida in 'The Law of Genre'. His hypothesis in its simplest and starkest form is this:

> ... a text would not *belong* to any genre. Every text *participates* in one or several genres, there is no genreless text, there is always a genre and genres, yet such participation never amounts to belonging.
>
> (Derrida 1980: 230)

The law of genre is 'a sort of participation without belonging – a taking part in without being part of, without having membership of a set' (Derrida 1980: 227). And the reason why a relationship of belonging is not possible is a logical one: the 'mark' that designates membership in a set (the word 'novel', for example) does not itself belong to that set, and may indeed be taken as an object of 'remark' (may be remarked upon) by a text within the set. It would thus occupy a position at once 'outside' the text, as a designation of its class, and 'inside' it as a content which is reflected upon. This logical paradox is what Derrida calls 'invagination', a folding in of the set upon itself (the word also plays with the opposition of nature and culture that is put in play by the biological roots of the word 'genre'); and the reflexivity that sustains this paradox is, he says, characteristic of 'what we call art, poetry or literature' (Derrida 1980: 229). These are the forms of writing which are at once marked by genre and perpetually at work upon it, internalising and thereby transforming its 'rules'.

Rules, law, genre as law: as soon as the word 'genre' is sounded, says Derrida, 'a limit is drawn. And when a limit is established, norms and interdictions are not far behind: "Do," "Do not" ' (Derrida 1980: 224). The law of genre is a law of purity, a law against miscegenation. Yet lodged at the heart of this law is another, 'a law of impurity or a principle of contamination' (Derrida 1980: 225) which registers the impossibility of *not* mixing genres. The tension between these two principles is given by the fact of **repetition** or **citation**: the fact that any text (for example, the two sentences with which Derrida begins his essay, and which he then modifies slightly by repetition) can be shifted from its generic context and placed in another, or the difficulty of distinguishing a citation from a non-citation. The law of genre is from the very beginning undermined by its lack of hold over the texts which it seems to regulate; genre, the law of genre as 'order's principle' is countered by 'the madness of genre' (Derrida 1980: 252), by the fact that 'there is no madness without the law' (Derrida 1980: 251), no law without madness.

Yet to put the matter this way is to suppose that genre is, in the first place, and however much it is from the very beginning undermined, a matter of law. Against its limits, its closure, its injunction to purity is then set the wildness of literature, of writings, like the Blanchot story Derrida reads in the rest of his essay, which set the schematic classifications of genre theory spinning. But all this depends on the initial decision to view genre as a principle of taxonomic purity, something like the folk theory of categorisation I mentioned earlier. As Freadman puts it, 'Derrida's paradox holds for just those genre statements that are made according to the Aristotelian model of genre theory, i.e. class-names asserted positively' (Freadman 1986: 363).

For all its productive ambivalence, Derrida's argument participates in (I won't say 'belongs to') a familiar post-Romantic resistance to genre understood as a prescriptive taxonomy and as a constraint on textual energy. What matters about the literary text is its singularity: in Friedrich Schlegel's words, which in a sense initiate this tradition around the end of the eighteenth century, *Die modernen Dichtarten sind nur Eine oder unendlich viele. Jedes Gedicht eine Gattung für sich*: the modern genres are either just One or an endless **multiplicity**; every work is its own genre, is *sui generis*

(Schlegel 1957: 116). On the one hand, then, the irreducibility of text to system: for Benedetto Croce, writing a century after the brothers Schlegel, aesthetic or intuitive modes of thinking are antithetical to logical or scientific modes, and genre theory, the 'theory of artistic and literary kinds', makes the error of trying 'to deduce the expression from the concept, and to find in what takes its place the laws of the thing whose place is taken' (Croce 2000: 27). The aesthetic has no logic, logic kills aesthetic expression. For the deconstructionist Thomas Keenan, writing another century later, the heart of the literary experience is 'our exposure to the singularity of a text, something that cannot be organised in advance, whose complexities cannot be settled or decided by "theories" or the application of more or less mechanical programs' (Keenan 1997: 1). But of course our experience of a text always is organised in advance – by expectations about what *kind* of text it is, if nothing else.

On the other hand, however, this absolute singularity of the Book is at the same time an absolute generality, that of literature. Maurice Blanchot takes this tradition of resistance to genre to its logical extreme when he writes:

> The only thing that matters is the book, just as it is, far from genres, outside the rubrics – prose, poetry, novel, first-person account – under which it refuses to place itself and to which it denies the power of fixing it in its place and determining its form. A book no longer belongs to a genre, every book arises only from literature, as if the latter possessed in advance, in their generality, the secrets and formulae which alone permit to be given to what is written the reality of a book. Everything would thus take place as if, the genres having been dissipated, literature alone were affirmed, ... as though there were, then, an 'essence' of literature.
>
> (Blanchot 1959: 293, my translation)

This is what Philippe Lacoue-Labarthe and Jean-Luc Nancy (1988), paraphrasing and extrapolating from Schlegel, call the Literary Absolute, literature not as one genre or another but as at once the totality and the dissolution of kinds.

One possible response to this tradition is to see it, as Michel Beaujour does, as a way of sacralising literature, turning it into a transcendental category which can have no truck with the profane realities of the 'discursive functions and **speech acts** embodied in all kinds of utterances', including the 'multiplicity of genres' (Beaujour 1980: 18). Yet I want to argue that the post-Romantic resistance to genre is not in any simple way 'wrong'. On the contrary, it seems to me important to stress the open-endedness of genres and the irreducibility of texts to a single interpretive framework. Derrida is right to distinguish between participation and belonging, and to argue that the 'participation' of texts in genres cannot mean a subsumption of the members of a class in the closed totality to which they belong. Texts work upon genres as much as they are shaped by them, genres are open-ended sets, and participation in a genre takes many different forms.

At the same time, no text is ever unframed, even if it is the case that the act of citation or of translation or merely survival from one moment in time to another all alter the generic framework within which texts are read. Texts and genres exist in an unstable relation, but at any one moment this relation is 'stabilised-for-now' or 'stabilised-enough' (Schryer 1994: 107). Even when a text disrupts all the expectations we may have of it, these expectations nevertheless form the ways in which we can read it and the ways in which we can change our minds (that is, develop new expectations). As the German literary theorist H.R. Jauss (1982: 79) puts it:

> [j]ust as there is no act of verbal communication that is not related to a general, socially or situationally conditioned norm or convention, it is also unimaginable that a literary work set itself into an informational vacuum, without indicating a specific situation of understanding. To this extent, every work belongs to a genre...

and genre matters to the reading of every text.

2

SIMPLE AND COMPLEX GENRES

SIMPLE FORMS: THE RIDDLE

Some genres seem rather simple, others very complex. Some are closely anchored to a particular kind of situation, others seem to float free of any such grounding. Some are close to, or even identical with, a single speech act, as is the prayer to praying, the military command to ordering, while others such as the novel or the shaggy-dog story are made up of a multiplicity of speech acts and can incorporate a wide range of other genres.

For these reasons, a number of writers have made a theoretical distinction between simple and complex genres, or between 'fundamental' forms and the more elaborate forms built from them. André Jolles describes nine 'simple forms' which are the ancestors of the developed literary genres. Andrew Welsh explores the 'roots of lyric' in riddles, charms, and chants, which he takes to correspond to the three fundamental forms of poetry defined by Pound: *melopoeia* (musical), *phanopoeia* (visual), and *logopoeia* ('the dance of intellect among words') (Welsh 1978: 15). The Russian theorist V.N. Volosinov, who was part of the circle around Mikhail Bakhtin in the 1920s and 1930s and whose published work may in part have been authored by Bakhtin, writes of the 'little speech genres' of oral communication. Emphasising the importance of 'language etiquette, speech tact and other forms of adjusting an utterance to the hierarchical organisation of society', he argues that each period and each social class has a repertoire of 'ways of speaking' in particular kinds of situation, where the content of utterances is adapted to a particular form of utterance (Volosinov 1973: 21). Bakhtin picks up the argument in one of his late essays. Speech genres, he says, are tied to particular 'spheres of activity', and each such sphere 'contains an entire repertory of speech genres that differentiate and grow as the particular sphere develops and becomes more complex' (Bakhtin 1986: 60). The notion of complexity, and the distinction between primary and secondary genres, are central to his analysis:

> Secondary (complex) speech genres – novels, dramas, all kinds of scientific research, major genres of commentary, and so forth – arise in more complex and comparatively highly developed and organised cultural communication (primarily written) that is artistic, scientific, sociopolitical, and so on. During the process of their formation, they absorb and digest various primary (simple) genres that have taken form in unmediated speech communication. These primary genres are altered and assume a special character when they enter into complex ones. They lose their immediate relation to actual reality and to the real utterances of others.
>
> (Bakhtin 1986: 62)

The distinction can be extended beyond verbal texts. Architecture, for example, can be thought of as working with a small range of simple types such as the hut, the cottage, the fortified keep, the store room, the cell, the temple, which form the basis for all of its more sophisticated and complex forms, and to which it constantly refers. This is interesting not because it allows us to reduce the complex to the simple, but because the simple forms tend to have specific and definite meanings or functions which are then extended, expanded, aggregated, parodied or in some other way transformed in the more complex forms.

I begin this chapter by testing out some of these assumptions against one of Jolles's nine 'simple forms', the riddle, a genre which seems to be universally distributed and to range from simple children's games to an elaborate literary form. The riddle is 'fundamental' in the sense that it works as a basic **language game** built on the social dynamics of question and answer, or challenge and response, and explores these dynamics through the control of an enigmatic or hidden knowledge. It is close to some of the most basic **figures** of speech, especially catachresis (the application of a term to a thing which it does not properly denote, as in 'the leg of a table') and metaphor, but it does have an elaborated literary form and it seems to give shape to a number of other genres, such as the Metaphysical lyric, the Malay *pantun*, the Baroque emblem, or detective fiction. It is of considerable antiquity: the oldest recorded riddles, written in Sumerian with Assyrian translations, come from ancient Babylon some 2000 years before the Christian era (Taylor 1976: 13):

> You went and took the enemy's property;
> The enemy came and took your property.
> > (a shuttle)

> Who becomes pregnant without conceiving,
> Who becomes fat without eating?
> > (a rain cloud)

These are recognisably riddles in their posing of a puzzle formed by the description of an unknown object which has to be guessed. Although the first of these Sumerian riddles is not in the form of a question and answer, it can easily be rewritten in terms of the underlying structure: 'What is the name of that thing which ...?', that we – 'we' in Western **modernity** – take to be the canonical form of the riddle.

Yet it is perhaps too simple to suppose that riddles are universally cast in a common form. Not all question-and-answer texts are riddles. A number of African texts classed as riddles may strike us as anomalous. Lee Haring (1985: 165) cites the following:

> perfume from the forest (ginger)
> the grease [fat] of wood (honey)

Since they have only one **predicate**, in that they say only one thing about the object they describe, rather than two, these utterances seem to work as metaphors, lacking the element of paradox or wit that we tend to associate with riddles. Again, some Malagasy riddles simply describe the features of a well-known place:

> perched high where there are beautiful shadows
> (Ambohimanga)

This is barely more than a literal statement, akin to certain 'non-oppositional riddles' cited by Georges and Dundes (1963: 114) ('Wha / live in de river? Fish'). Other forms of riddle-like statement that we tend to distinguish from the 'true' riddle are catechismic questions, where the answers are derived from bodies of doctrine rather than involving wit; the Zen *koan*, the point of which is to achieve enlightenment rather than to find a solution; quiz questions about specialised bodies of knowledge like sport, where the answer involves recall rather than ingenuity; and the so-called 'neck riddle', a form in which the questioner's life depends on defeating his executioner with an unanswerable riddle – and where it is the impossibility of the answer, because of what seems like the arbitrariness of its relation to the question, that defines this as a variant form (Perpicello and Green 1984: 87). Consider the most famous of all neck riddles, the one posed by Samson to the Philistines (*Judges* 14):

> Out of the eater came forth meat, and out of the strong came
> forth sweetness.
>   (honey from bees swarming in the carcase of a lion)

The sense of paradox centring on two sets of opposed ideas: eating meat and supplying meat, strength and sweetness, is strong here, but the paradox is designed not to entice but to defeat an answer. The passage between these predicates and the riddle's highly particular referent (honey in a lion's carcase) is too distant and too difficult for us to feel that Samson is playing fair.

The poles of literalness and arbitrariness define the ways in which riddles can be unsatisfactory: a 'good' riddle must be ingenious (not literal) and yet, at least potentially, answerable (not arbitrary). The fact that we have so strong a sense of what is *not* a well-formed riddle is a strong indication that our modern, Western understanding of the genre conforms to certain basic rules, certain presuppositions about both the form and the content of the genre. Let me now try to spell out some of them.

A riddle presents an enigma. Or rather, the enigma is presented by the questioner as a challenge to the one questioned: the question, or the initial statement, offers something hidden from understanding, but which is understood by the speaker. This 'something' is both present and absent.

Suppose a very basic riddle:

What has eyes but can't see? (potato)

The question contains two predicates that posit two things about the unknown referent: that X has eyes; and that X cannot see. The possession of eyes is normally something we associate with faces, and one possible answer to this question would be 'the face of a blind person'. But this answer would be less than satisfying, because it is literal, and because it is a little too obvious. The answer 'potato' is neater, and it activates the pun on the word 'eye' in a way that produces an elementary form of wit. (Again, the word 'eye' is an example of catachresis.)

The presence of two possible answers, one obvious and wrong, and one that is correct but not obvious, is a feature of many riddles. Alternatively, instead of an obvious but wrong answer there may simply be a block, an insoluble puzzle. The enigma at the core of any riddle has to do with its exploitation of 'the ambiguity of words and the multiplicity of conceptual relations' (Freud 1960, quoted in Hamnett 1967: 382). More precisely, it relies on the fact that any noun carries with it a set of predicates, a set of qualities that we normally associate with it, such as eyes with faces; and on the fact that such predicate-sets may partially overlap: both faces and potatoes have 'eyes'; both clouds and pregnant women are 'swollen'. The riddle selects properties which seem most plausibly to belong to X but which may also belong to Y, and it often makes it clear through the use of a paradoxical tension between two or more properties that X is not the underlying referent. The 'work' of the riddle involves a crafted play with the overlap between these predicate-sets.

The riddle has two parts, often but not necessarily a question and an answer, spoken by two different people; and these two parts have a common referent. They are synonyms, have a common core of meaning; and this core is conveyed in a relation of symbolisation which is organised by a range of rhetorical figures both at the semantic level and at the level of sound. This is the reason why catechism questions don't count as riddles: the question and the answer are not synonymous. Tzvetan Todorov thus defines the riddle as the unity within a **dialogic** couplet of a predicate and a **subject**: a set of properties, and the thing they describe. Taken together, this dialogue of subject and predicate gives a *definition* of the thing, either of the kind you would find in a dictionary or of the kind you would find in an encyclopaedia, and definitions are pieces of 'public' knowledge which must be sharable. This is why answers known only to an individual, like Samson's riddle, are not appropriate to the 'true' riddle (Todorov 1978: 228–9).

The underlying form of the riddle is thus something like this:

1   This thing has eyes
2   This thing cannot see
3   What is this thing?
4   Answer (a): this thing is the face of a blind person
5   Answer (b): this thing is a potato

Yet is it true that riddles have only two parts, corresponding to a question (1–3) and an answer (4 or 5)? In one sense, yes: this is how riddles are represented in written form. But in practice the answer is frequently *not* given by the person questioned, and is rather the last of three moves, which Goffman characterises as '(1) question, (2) thought and give-up, (3) answer' (Goffman 1981: 54). It is, normatively, the *questioner* who supplies the answer after defeating his or her interlocutor. In order to account for this discrepancy between two different ways of understanding the riddle, we need now to think about it in terms of the social practice in which it is embedded, the action it performs within a framework of social interaction, and that helps to shape its inner dynamic.

In these terms, the riddle can be understood as a verbal contest staged over a hidden knowledge. Enacting a duel between two or more interlocutors, it passes from enigma to revelation and conversational victory and defeat. In two variant forms, the duel saves the life of the questioner (the neck riddle) or saves the life of the person answering (the oedipal riddle, the archetype of which is Oedipus's escape from his encounter with the Sphinx by guessing the answer to her riddling question). Describing it as a charm (a magical spell) in reverse, Northrop Frye characterises the riddle as a trap that can be sprung if we guess the right answer, whereas the unguessed or unguessable riddle may destroy us (Frye 1976: 136). Thus, 'riddles often imply some kind of enmity-situation or contest, where you will lose a great deal, perhaps your life, if you don't know the answer' (Frye 1976: 137).

It is insufficient, then, to think of the riddle solely as a verbal form. It is, more broadly, a **discursive practice** which constructs a certain kind of relationship between its protagonists. Traces of the sacred or taboo hang around the secret knowledge possessed by the questioner (Caillois 1986: 151), and the challenge and response built into the structure of question and answer encode the form of a ritual ordeal. This is elegantly indicated *a contrario* in the form of Swahili riddle interaction reported by Kallen and Eastman, where the 'answer' takes the form of a story in which both the riddle-giver and the recipients are given the solution by an old woman. This solving of the puzzle by a third party 'de-emphasises the divisive elements originally present in the riddle interchange, and softens the blow to the riddle recipients who could not themselves supply the knowledge required of them' (Kallen and Eastman 1979: 423).

If the riddle is a form of verbal contest, what is the effect of giving a correct answer to the riddle question? Here is another riddle that has something to say about this:

> When one does not know what it is, then it is something; but when one knows what it is, then it is nothing.
>
> (Taylor 1976: 4)

The 'it' here is the riddle itself: riddles lose their point when they are solved. Goffman agrees:

> The purpose of the asked person's move is not to inform the asker about the answer but to show whether he is smart enough to uncover what the asker already knows. But here the interaction falls flat if indeed the correct answer is uncovered ... or if, upon being told the

answer, the asked person does not do an appreciable 'take', this latter constituting a fourth move.

(Goffman 1981: 54)

Thus riddles should have one good solution, and this solution, just as in the detective story, should be both in principle available to the respondent, and in practice not available. This formal requirement shapes the kind of interaction the genre makes possible: the work that is done by riddles is that of linking people together around a game of knowing and not-knowing. (Again, I should stress that these rules apply only to the 'Western' form of the riddle: in some African forms the respondent's approach is governed by the fact that 'the connection between question and answer is fixed by tradition and popular acceptance' (Haring 1974: 197).)

What I have described thus far is, on the one hand, a logical structure which I take to be characteristic of the Western riddle, what Scott (1965: 74) calls a 'partially obscured semantic fit' between a subject and a set of predicates, and, on the other, a structure of **enunciation** which has to do with a stylised contest between questioner and respondent, waged as a struggle for possession of a secret or hidden knowledge. These are both dimensions of the presentation of an enigma, and they are central to the social meaning of the riddle; a third dimension has to do with the thematic content of riddles.

Of course, riddles can be about anything. We can guess from their frequent occurrence as children's games that they have something to do with learning about the basic categories of the world, in part by upsetting them, playing around with them; and perhaps the majority of the world's riddles refer to the ordinary things of daily use. Archer Taylor's exhaustive *English Riddles from Oral Tradition* groups the content of riddles as: living creatures, animals, persons, plants, things, and the form, function, colour or acts of these entities (Taylor 1951). But in the more elaborate riddles of literary and folkloric tradition, certain *topoi* (recurrent topics of discourse) which are embryonically present in the simpler forms tend to emerge as characteristic. I identify three of them: 'thingness'; sexuality; and the disorder of nature.

The first two of these themes can be neatly identified through their fusion in a number of literary riddles from the Anglo-Saxon corpus, notably the collection of riddles in the tenth-century *Exeter Book*. Descended from the late-Latin genre of the *aenigma*, the riddle – often cast in the first-person: *Ic eom* or *Ic waes*, I am, I was – emerges in English 'as the enigmatic voice of certain highly wrought objects', with close affinities to the inscriptions found on crosses, weapons, bells, sundials, chess pieces and so on; the riddle is the voice of the object, 'withhold[ing] the name of a thing so that the thing may appear as what it is not, in order to be revealed for what it is' (Tiffany 2001: 73, 79). But consider riddle number 44 in Muir's edition of the *Exeter Book*, in my translation:

> A curious thing hangs   by a man's thigh
> Full under the cloth.   It is pierced in front.
> It is stiff and hard   and it stands proud;
> When the man pulls up   his garment
> Over his knees   he wants to poke
> With the head of his hanging thing   that well-known hole
> That he has often   filled before.
>   (key)

> (Muir 2000: 322–3)

Here the descriptive detail is developed for its own sake, emphasising the material thingness of this object; the initial word *wraetlic*, which occurs in a number of other riddles in the *Exeter Book* and which I have translated as 'a curious thing', comes from a word meaning an ornament, a jewel, or a work of art, and it has the sense of something skilfully wrought, hence wondrous, curious, or rare. Yet this descriptive detail is at the same time a functional part of the poem's game of misleading the reader into supposing a sexual content. Sexuality, the private parts of the body (a theme that recurs throughout the *Exeter Book* riddles) is in one sense the exemplary form of hidden or secret knowledge. These riddles suggest that a concern with the details of thingness is also a form of sexual curiosity, and the riddle form is perhaps ideally suited to exploring it.

The other thematic area that I find characteristic of the riddle is bound up with the formal centrality of paradox to its display of enigma. It works as a statement of simultaneous being and not being, as in the following (unanswered) riddle from the *Palatine Anthology* (cited in Taylor 1951: 302): 'No one sees me when he sees, but he sees me when he sees not; he who speaks does not speak, and he who runs does not run, and I am untruthful though I tell all truth'. A Jamaican riddle similarly plays with negation:

> A man have a corn field and he says, 'If they come, they won't come; and if they don't come, they come'. The king ask him the meaning of that. He tell him, 'If your pigeons come, your corn won't come; and if your pigeons don't come, your corn will come'.
>
> (Abrahams 1985: 87)

The more striking form of this accentuation of paradox in the riddle occurs, however, in the thematisation of an *inverted* or *ambiguous natural order*. A simple example is a group of riddles (Taylor 1951, nos. 806–15) which turn the eating of fruit into a violently murderous act. This (following Taylor's numbering system) is 806a:

> As I went over London Bridge,
> I saw a lady standing;
> I pulled off her head and sucked her blood
> And left her body standing.
>   (blackberry)

It is above all in the neck riddle, however, that the force of negation and the thematisation of natural disorder most powerfully occur. This is the motif of 'pregnant death':

> As I walked out and in again,
> From the dead the living came.
> Six there is and seven there'll be,
> So tell me this riddle and set me free.
>   (A horse's skull in which he has seen a bird hatching its brood of seven, with one still hatching)
>
> (Dorst 1983: 419)

And this is the motif of posthumous birth:

> Under the earth I go,
> Upon oak leaves I stand;

I ride on a filly that never was foaled,
And carry the mare's skin in my hand.

> (The man had put earth in his cap, oak leaves in his shoe,
> cut open a pregnant mare to obtain the foal, and made a whip of
> the mare's skin)

(Dorst 1983: 426)

Finally, Dorst cites a group of neck riddles having to do with a hero conceived incestuously between a father and a daughter. The hero is cut from his mother's womb, either causing her death or following upon her murder. Later, he obtains a horse that is also 'unborn'. In some cases gloves are made from the mother's skin. The hero eventually wins a princess with a riddle alluding to his aberrant birth, the confusion of family relations in incest, and the gruesome article of clothing:

I am not born, neither is my horse. I am the son of the daughter of
my father, and I wear the hands of my mother.

(Dorst 1983: 428)

This whole thematic area has been particularly important in complex literary texts: in Lear's 'Nothing will come of nothing' (in Shakespeare's *King Lear*), or in the witches' prophetic riddle forecasting that 'none of woman born / Shall harm Macbeth' (*Macbeth*, IV, 1, 80–1) – a riddle answered by Macduff:

Despair thy charm;
And let the Angel, whom thou still has served,
Tell thee, Macduff was from his mother's womb
Untimely ripp'd.

(*Macbeth*, V, 8, 13–16)

Where the riddle explores natural disorder as an extension of its fascination with logical contradiction or ambiguity, and treats it in the same way as it does sexual innuendo or delight in the elaborately wrought thingness of things, the Shakespearean texts turn this fascination into a coherent metaphorical focus. The 'dark night' that 'strangles the travelling lamp', the falcon 'towering in her pride of place' which is 'hawk'd at, and kill'd' by 'a mousing owl', Duncan's horses which 'flung out, / Contending 'gainst obedience, as they would make/ War with mankind' and which 'eat each other' (*Macbeth* II, 4, 12–18) represent that more general disorder in language or in the natural world which is the counterpart of a tear in the social order of things. Yet the very richness of this metaphorical focus is in part made possible by the generic structures of the riddle on which *Macbeth* draws. The riddle is in one sense a 'simple' form but it is also a complex working of its raw materials: the logic of subject and predicate, the cultural organisation of the categories of being, the agonistic dynamics of question and answer, and the social force of the secret. It is only the beginning of an analysis to posit a distinction between simple and complex forms; however useful this distinction may be heuristically, all simple forms are in the long run complex.

GENERIC COMPLEXITY

Let me say, putting it very simply and continuing with this heuristic and provisional distinction, that a 'primary' genre is univocal: it speaks in its own 'voice', its formal logic is singular; whereas the more complex 'secondary' genres are multivocal: their formal logic allows or encourages the incorporation of other forms, other 'voices'. The prophetic riddles in *Macbeth* have an intertextual force: that is, they refer to the genres of prophecy and riddle, and actualise something of the semantic potential of each. From the prophecy they take the sense of an inevitable fate; from the riddle, the structure of an apparent paradox which is resolved in an unexpected way, as well as the link between patterns of order and disorder in language and in the natural world. By welding these two forms together, the play fuses the 'non-time' of the riddle (Dorst 1983: 423) with the prophecy's drive towards the future: from being a static, non-narrative form, the riddle here becomes dynamic; and the delivery of the answer to a question we had not suspected to be one ('What is the man who is not born of woman?') comes to work as a crucial moment of plot-reversal.

The play thus takes the two genres, prophecy and riddle, into itself, enriching its own texture by drawing upon their structural force. But what does it mean for our understanding of genre to say that a text in one genre incorporates a text in another, and what are the conditions that make this possible?

In order to begin formulating an answer to these questions, I want to look more closely at the concept of the *speech situation* and the relation of 'voices' within it. I take it that all human communication is in some sense grounded in and can be derived from a base form of face-to-face conversational exchange between two interlocutors: that is, that dialogue (not monologue) is the model of all human speech. In this situation, each speaker figures him- or herself as 'I' and their interlocutor as 'you'. Each of these pronouns is a representation of the presence of the speaker to themselves and to each other, but each of these pronouns also has the capacity to represent each person in situations other than the present one. Thus I can say that 'I was unhappy yesterday', meaning that 'I (here and now)' am speaking of myself ('I then') as other than my present self, just as 'you will be in Paris tomorrow' projects the present 'you' into a 'you' imagined in another time and place.

This basic speech situation thus already looks rather complex as a result of this capacity of the 'I' and the 'you' to represent both a present and an absent figure, or both present and absent aspects of the same figure. It is further complicated when we notice that these pronouns have a shifting reference: they are not names attached to bodies, but labile designations of places from which and to which to speak. Every person is 'I' to themselves and takes their interlocutor for a 'you', and these positions are fully reversible. With the addition of the third major slot in the speech situation, the third-person 'he' or 'she', however, an asymmetry is introduced: this other person is a silent participant, an object rather than a subject of speech, and is thus sometimes designated as a grammatical non-person, unless of course they too become an interlocutor, an 'I' or a 'you'. Thus the full speech situation consists of two or more interlocutors and a third, of whom they may speak; yet each interlocutor may speak of themselves (of 'I' and 'you') as though they too were such a third party, both present to and absent from the here and now of speech.

From this structural fact flows another: that every piece of speaking may embed another piece of speaking. I can cite myself or you or another person as speaking, at another time and place (whether real or fictive), in the first person: 'He said to me "I don't understand".' A *secondary* speech situation is thus embedded in the *primary* speech situation, and in principle this embedding could go on forever. The embedded speech may be directly reported, or it may be fully subsumed within the speaker's voice ('He said he didn't understand'), or it may be present only as a tonal inflection in that voice ('He didn't understand!').

The structure of enunciation in conversational exchange thus involves three different ways in which the *self-of-speech* (the 'I' and the 'you', the *subject of utterance*) is displaced and distinguished from the *actual people who speak* (the utterers, or *subjects of enunciation*): the speaker may refer to him- or herself, or to their interlocutor, as being in another place and time; the 'I' and 'you' of the speaking selves shift between speakers; and other speaking selves may be embedded in any act of speech. The selves operating in any speech situation are projections in language rather than empirical actualities. Goffman calls them 'enacted capacities' (Goffman 1981: 46), and talks of the personal pronoun as 'a figure in a statement' (147) which represents us to others, and others to us.

We tend to assume, nevertheless, that the statements I make when I speak are fully authored by me: that I am their sole source, even though I speak, to paraphrase Derrida (1976: 158), in a language and a logic which I did not invent and cannot fully control, and even if my speech is full of citations of the language of others. But this assumption supposes that language consists of statements isolated from each other. If, on the contrary, we accept that language mostly happens in the form of dialogue, then any statement is to some degree a response to another: whether I am replying to you, or merely anticipating your response to my statement, what I say will to some extent incorporate your actual or expected counter-statement. It inflects my speech, which in turn is 'accompanied by a continual sideways glance at another person' (Bakhtin 1984: 32).

This is a constant theme in Bakhtin's writing: language is *internally* shaped by its dialogic orientation. Any utterance is characterised by what he calls its 'addressivity' (Bakhtin 1986: 95), and thus exists in 'a dialogically agitated and tension-filled environment of alien words, value-judgements and accents, weaves in and out of complex interrelationships, merges with some, recoils from others, intersects with yet a third group ...' (Bakhtin 1981: 276). Even a single word may be heard dialogically if it is perceived 'not as the impersonal word of language but as a sign of someone else's semantic position, as the representative of another person's utterance; that is, if we hear in it someone else's voice' (Bakhtin 1984: 184). Language *in use* (that is, discourse) is filled with the dialogic play of speech acts and the meanings that attach to them.

Reported speech is, for Bakhtin and for Volosinov, the primordial example of this active, tension-filled play of speech-positions within discourse. Reported speech is at once 'speech within speech, utterance within utterance', and at the same time 'speech about speech, utterance about utterance' (Volosinov 1973: 115). A reported statement is thematised by and within its **context** but retains its difference, entering the syntactic field of the embedding sentence without surrendering its own syntactic and semantic integrity. Even when its syntax is modified, as in indirect discourse ('He said he didn't understand') or free indirect discourse ('He didn't understand!' – where only the intonational traces of the reported statement remain), it holds on to something of its semantic and even its constructional autonomy. And the reason why this is important is that 'what is expressed in the forms employed for reporting speech is an *active relation* of one message to another, and it is expressed, moreover, not on the level of the theme but in the stabilised constructional patterns of the language itself' (Volosinov 1973: 116). Study of the forms of reported speech has theoretical precedence even over the study of dialogue, because 'these forms reflect basic and constant tendencies in the *active reception of other speakers' speech*', something which is fundamental as well for dialogue (Volosinov 1973: 117).

It is this focus on the dialogic play of utterances that leads to Bakhtin's later concern with the integration and thematisation of other *genres* within the genre of the novel, and which has given us the most extended account we have of the processes by which metageneric forms of discourse are constructed. The novel is his privileged model of a complex secondary genre:

> To a greater or lesser extent, every novel is a dialogised system made up of the images of 'languages', styles and consciousnesses that are concrete and inseparable from language. Language in the novel not only represents, but itself serves as the object of representation.
>
> (Bakhtin 1981: 49)

What the novel gives us, through such technical devices as free indirect discourse and the use of 'intonational quotation marks', is 'the image of another's language and outlook on the world, simultaneously represented *and* representing' (Bakhtin 1981: 45). Its discourse is 'double-voiced', directed 'both toward the referential object of speech ... and toward *another's discourse*, toward *someone else's* speech' (Bakhtin 1984: 185). Incorporating such genres as the confession, the diary, the letter, travel notes, and biography, the novel processes these generic forms as '"frames" or "fixes" on the world':

> Each of these genres possesses its own verbal and semantic forms for assimilating various aspects of reality. The novel, indeed, utilises these genres precisely because of their capacity, as well worked-out forms, to assimilate reality in words.
>
> (Bakhtin 1981: 320–1)

Indeed, the novel is so dependent on other genres that it itself 'has the appearance of being merely a secondary syncretic unification of other seemingly primary verbal genres' (Bakhtin 1981: 321). It is more like a fusion of other genres than a genre in its own right, but this is precisely what gives it its force: in absorbing 'voices' from the culture, the novel activates the reality-forming dimensions of genre. The key Bakhtin coinage here is '**heteroglossia**', the orientation towards a multiplicity of other voices and languages which so marks the stylistics of the novel and which is realised through a range of stylised vocalisations:

> Authorial speech, the speeches of narrators, inserted genres, the speech of characters are merely those fundamental compositional unities with whose help heteroglossia can enter the novel; each of them permits a multiplicity of social voices and a wide variety of their links and interrelationships.
>
> (Bakhtin 1981: 263)

Heteroglossia is not just a matter of the incorporation and stylisation of other genres, then: it covers the full range of citation of other speech forms and of the play between different **positions of enunciation**. Yet insofar as other genres appear in the novel *in the form of* 'voices', complexes of ways of speaking and subject matter, these different levels of structure are treated equivalently by the novel. 'Voices', enunciative positions, are the modalities in which generic formations become recognisable in the novel. My interest here, however, is not in the stylistics of the novel as such; indeed, it is arguable that Bakhtin makes too much of the particularity of the novel form, separating it too sharply from what he thinks of as the more monologic genres of epic, drama and poetry. My interest, rather, lies in the ways in which any 'complex' genre – and this would include everyday conversation, perhaps the most 'basic' of all speech forms – is built out of allusions to and stylisations of other genres, and constructs its authority and credibility on this basis.

CITATION AND INTERTEXTUALITY

The organising logic of genre, its patterns of meaning, of form, and of enunciation, is *represented* and *enacted* by pieces of text. The cryptic riddle form embedded in 'none of woman born / Shall harm Macbeth' – really a concealed question to which the answer is 'Macduff was from his mother's womb / Untimely ripp'd' – is presented to us by way of this particular *instance* of the genre. Indeed, this is the only way we know about the structures of genre: through particular texts from which we extrapolate a more general logic.

The embedding of the logic of one genre within the logic of another takes place textually, then; and the general process of which I have been speaking could perhaps be called *citation*: that is, the shifting of text from one textual and generic context to another. Reported speech is one example of this; allusion to a genre is another. Briggs and Bauman (1992: 141) give the example of the Kuna people's curing texts called *irkarkana* (from the Panamanian territory of San Blas) which are discussed by the anthropologist Joel Sherzer. Their uses range:

> from the primary magical uses for curing, disease prevention, improving abilities, and general control of the spirit world to the rehearsal of an *ikar* by specialists, the teaching and learning of an *ikar*, and the chanting of an *ikar* for entertainment on festive occasions, each of which is marked by formal and functional differences.

And of course the *ikar* can also be cited as a piece of ethnographic evidence, or as an example of the uses of genre. Such shift of context is a normal and central part of human language, and it is one of the reasons why there is no simple fit between a text and a genre. Yet much of the logic of genre survives these translations from one context to another. A letter inserted into a third-person narrative retains the structure of first-person speech, together with its connotations of intimacy and directness, within the new speech situation that now frames it and gives it a different function. This is similar to Volosinov's point about reported speech retaining its semantic and even syntactic integrity within the embedding sentence (Volosinov 1973: 115–16). The embedded text has been 'keyed', to employ a useful phrase of Erving Goffman's: shifted from a primary to a secondary framework which is patterned on the first but perceived to be quite different from it. Goffman's initial example of **keying**, borrowed from Bateson (1973), is of the way animals play by pretending to fight: what looks like hurtful and aggressive behaviour is in fact bracketed, suspended, so that 'bitinglike behaviour occurs, but no one is seriously bitten' (Goffman 1974: 41). Human behaviour is rich in analogous forms of bracketing: make-believe and fantasy, aesthetic activity more generally, contests and ceremonials, practising or replaying or rehearsing, and the 'regrounding' of an activity in a context where it means something quite different, such as work performed for charity. One definition of aesthetic practices is that they are keyings of the real: representations of real acts or thoughts or feelings which are not themselves, in the same sense, real. Shifting texts to another generic context has that kind of effect: it suspends the primary generic *force* of the text, but not its generic *structure*.

In the last chapter I quoted Miller's definition of genre as 'typified rhetorical actions based in recurrent situations' (Miller 1994a: 31). Now I need to add to this the qualification that, insofar as texts are constantly 'keyed', constantly cited in other contexts, they are thus constantly shifted out of the situation to which they typically respond. Take the following embedding of a letter in a narrative context (Austen 1966: 310):

> She had read Miss Crawford's note only once; and how to reply to any thing so imperfectly understood was most distressing. Quite unpractised in such sort of note-writing, had there been time for scruples and fears as to style, she would have felt them in abundance; but something must be instantly written, and with only one decided feeling, that of wishing not to appear to think anything really intended, she wrote thus, in great trembling both of spirits and hand:

'I AM very much obliged to you, my dear Miss Crawford, for your kind congratulations, as far as they relate to my dearest William. The rest of your note I know means nothing; but I am so unequal to any thing of the sort, that I hope you will excuse my begging you to take no further notice. I have seen too much of Mr Crawford not to understand his manners; if he understood me as well, he would, I dare say, behave differently. I do not know what I write, but it would be a great favour of you never to mention the subject again. With thanks for the honour of your note,

I remain, dear Miss Crawford,

&c. &c.'

The conclusion was scarcely intelligible from increasing fright, for she found that Mr Crawford, under pretence of receiving the note, was coming towards her.

In this passage from *Mansfield Park* the letter's 'primary' speech situation, as a mediated exchange between two people who are spatially separated and who engage in a socially tense but formally courteous negotiation about their personal relationship, is retained as an 'internal', structural dimension of its form, but it is at the same time subordinated to the third-person speech situation of the narrative where it works as a kind of symptomatic expression from which we can make a judgement about the heroine Fanny Price's handling of this situation. We see Fanny, that is to say, momentarily from the 'inside' (as indeed we do every time her speech is directly reported) before switching back to an 'external' view. From being a subject of speech in the letter, Fanny becomes an object of scrutiny, her 'character' integrated in the thematic patterning of the novel.

At the same time, however, it is precisely the generic characteristics of the letter as a form of social exchange which work here to structure the scene's dramatic irony. At this point in the novel Fanny is subject to moral pressure both from Henry Crawford, who wishes to marry her, and from his sister Mary. Seeking to avert the relationship which she feels is being forced on her, Fanny uses a medium which contradicts her message: she wishes to break off an exchange, the letter reinforces it. The same thing happens in Choderlos de Laclos's *Dangerous Liaisons* (1782), where a letter written by the Présidente to Valmont telling him she will have nothing to do with him is precisely a way of continuing their relationship (Laclos 1961: 210); or more extremely, when the Présidente keeps returning Valmont's letter which he recycles in new envelopes, the letter communicates as a pure fact of relationship rather than as a content.

Part of what the complex aesthetic genres imitate, then, is other genres and the effects they produce. In doing so they displace the genres they cite from their primary manner of producing these effects and turn them into a thematic object. They work – to quote Volosinov again – as 'speech about speech, utterance about utterance' (Volosinov 1973: 115).

A more general word than 'citation' for this phenomenon of speech (or writing, or images) which refers to other speech (or writing, or images ...) is *intertextuality*. What I mean by this is the range of processes by which a text invokes another, but also the way texts are constituted as such by their relationships with other texts. No text is unique; we could not recognise it if it were. All texts are relevantly similar to some texts and relevantly dissimilar to others. Similarity and difference form one pole of intertextual relations; citation, including implicit or explicit invocation, passing allusion, parody, and even at times the significant *absence* of reference to a text, forms another. All texts are shaped by the repetition and the transformation of other textual structures.

Genre is central to this process. Like reported speech, write Briggs and Bauman:

> genre is quintessentially intertextual. When discourse is linked to a particular genre, the process by which it is produced and received is mediated through its relationship with prior discourse. Unlike most examples of reported speech, however, the link is not made to isolated utterances, but to generalised or abstracted models of discourse production and reception.
>
> (Briggs and Bauman 1992: 147)

This is to say that intertextual reference works at different levels of generality. Texts may refer to other, quite specific texts; they may refer to structured pieces of language, such as proverbs or formulae or clichés; they may refer to a more general form of organisation of texts, such as genres or speech varieties or conventional plot structures; or they may refer to bodies of knowledge which do not have a specifically textual form.

The French critic Laurent Jenny has asked whether it is appropriate to apply the concept of intertextuality to references to a genre, since such a relation exists at the level of the code (the abstract organising system) rather than its textual realisation. But he immediately concedes that it is not possible to make a rigid distinction between the levels of code and text: 'Genre archetypes, however abstract, still constitute textual structures' (Jenny 1982: 42), and reference to a text implicitly invokes reference to the full set of potential meanings stored in the codes of the genre. It could be argued that Werner Herzog's film *Nosferatu: Phantom der Nacht* (1979) is so closely modelled on F.W. Murnau's precursor film (*Nosferatu: Eine Symphonie des Grauens*, 1922) that it cannot be fully understood without reference to it; but something, perhaps nearly everything, can be understood even if we have never seen Murnau's film, because what is crucial even in precisely repetitive films like Herzog's is that the precursor text belongs to a genre: its meanings never belong to it alone. The intertext, the precursor text, is never singular and never a moment of pure origin.

The remaking of one film by another gives a particularly clear insight into this crystallisation of the structure of a genre in a single text. To take another example, John Biguenet argues plausibly that *Home Alone* (1990) repeats a central feature of that genre of animated cartoons (the *Roadrunner* series, for example) in which plots are foiled and bodily hurt is reversible (Biguenet 1998: 140); it is the genre as a whole that the film assumes as its intertextual base, rather than any particular example of it (although one only needs to know a single example in order to 'know' the genre). Likewise, when *A Chorus Line* (1985) self-consciously remakes *Forty-Second Street* (1933), what is remade is both that movie and the genre of the 1930s Hollywood musical. But this repetition is not a simple continuity: as with nearly all remakes, the later film both picks up pieces of the former, knowingly integrating them into its own construction (the motif of the star's broken ankle which gives the newcomer her break, for example), and yet at the same time makes visible the historical distance between the two:

this is the world of the eighties, not the thirties. Cinematic remaking is a way of displaying the changes of a world through the changes in a genre, and it offers a compelling model of a practice which makes it impossible for us to think of texts as closed and self-contained bits of aesthetic substance.

3

LITERARY GENRE THEORY

GENRE AS TAXONOMY

Part of what it means to be a member of a culture is knowing the difference, and knowing how to talk about the difference, between riddles and jokes, tragedy and comedy, musicals and thrillers. Genre is, amongst other things, a matter of discrimination and taxonomy: of organising things into recognisable classes. In this respect it belongs to a much larger group of classifying activities that permeate every aspect of daily life, from informal and *ad hoc* ones like sorting out dirty dishes from clean ones, to more formalised ones like planning a meal or buying the right set of tools for a job. All of these activities involve the use of knowledges which are embedded in the flow of everyday practices.

Accounts of taxonomy tend to take as their **prototype** the powerful and rigorous models that have been developed in the sciences: the periodic table of the chemical elements, the Linnaean schema for organising the orders of the natural world, the Darwinian model of the evolution of species. We assume, according to Bowker and Star, that a workable system of classification has the following properties: first, 'there are consistent, unique classificatory principles in operation', such as atomic weight or genetic sequencing; second, 'the categories are mutually exclusive'; and third, 'the system is complete' (Bowker and Star 1999: 10–11). But no real-world system meets these requirements: in every system principles are mixed, and there are anomalies and ambiguities which the system sorts out as best it can.

We also tend to think of classifications as being like standards: explicit, formalised, durable rules which extend over several communities of practice. The **neoclassical** accounts of the literary genres that prevailed in Europe in much of the seventeenth and eighteenth centuries approached them in this spirit, as normative rules with universal validity rather than as *ad hoc*, changing, and inherently fuzzy practices. The equation of genres with systems of rules is one of a number of metaphors that have shaped the genre of genre theory. Exploring these metaphors, David Fishelov (1993: 1–2) speaks of four main sets of analogies through which twentieth-century critics have conceptualised the literary genres: the biological *species*; the *family*, and the resemblance between family members; the social *institution*, made up of conventions, norms, or contracts; and the *speech act*. Thomas Beebee (1994: 3) speaks of four stages of genre criticism since the Renaissance, in which genre is understood successively as *rules*, as organically developing *species*, as patterns of *textual features*, and as *conventions of reading*. And Rick Altman (1999: 14) sees the concept of genre in film theory working as a *blueprint* (the formulae governing production), as *structure* (the formal framework of the film), as a *label* (in marketing and distribution), and as a *contract* regulating relations with the audience.

To put this differently, and sticking with the magic number four, we could say that accounts of genre always draw on some other, authoritative realm for their metaphors, conceiving genre as a fact of language, as a sociological fact, as a matter of social etiquette, or as something like the natural organism. In each case the metaphor provides a way of thinking systematically about a form of ordering that is in many ways resistant to system.

It has been above all the model of the biological species, building on the organic connotations of the concepts of 'kind' and 'genre', that has been used to bring the authority of a scientific discourse to genre theory. Ferdinand Brunetière's *Evolution of Genres in Literary History* (1890) is the key text here, but the structural model of the relation of a species to the taxonomic levels above and beneath it, and of the internal uniformity and closure of the species, permeates the whole field. Altman writes of it as follows:

Reinvented by virtually every student of genre since Brunetière, scientific justification of genre study serves to convince theorists that genres actually exist, that they have distinct borders, that they can be firmly identified, that they operate systematically, that their internal functioning can be observed and scientifically described, and that they evolve according to a fixed and identifiable trajectory.

(Altman 1999: 6)

In practice, none of this is particularly useful for thinking about the literary or other kinds, for the good reason that genres are facts of culture which can only with difficulty be mapped onto facts of nature. Specifically, we can make the following objections to the biological model of species and evolution: first, the morphology of any genre is open-ended and indeterminate in comparison with the biological species, because it involves no genetic continuity; second, whereas the biological genus is defined by the fact that it is not interfertile with another genus, in the case of the discursive kinds 'not only are all genres interfertile, they may at any time be crossed with any genre that ever existed' (Altman 1999: 70); and third, whereas in biology the individual organism 'can only manifest or exemplify the group', in literature and in culture more generally every individual text 'to some extent modifies or changes the group' (Fishelov 1993: 21). Conversely, therefore, the properties of the text cannot be directly or simply derived from its genre. As Schaeffer puts it:

When we seek to elucidate the relationship of the *Aeneid* to the epic, the question we ask ourselves is not that of its belonging to the class as it may be defined once the *Aeneid* is a part of it, but that of its shaping force, the shaping force that is precisely one of the reasons the class such as we know it today possesses one appearance rather than another.

(Schaeffer 1989: 74)

The model of taxonomy that I have called 'Aristotelian' assumes that there can be something like an exhaustive classification which can 'place any member of a given population into one and only one class' (Bowker and Star 1999: 62). Other models of classification seek to address the fuzziness and open-endedness of the relation between texts and genres. Alastair Fowler, for example, proposes a Wittgensteinian logic of 'family resemblance', according to which 'representatives of a genre may then be regarded as making up a possible class whose septs [clans or classes] and individual members are related in various ways, without necessarily having any single feature shared in common by all' (Fowler 1982: 41). But using likeness as the basis for a classification raises the problem of where the line of *dis*similarity is to be drawn: 'how is one to decide that family resemblance does *not* exist?' (Miner 1986: 24). Fowler addresses the same question when he criticises Wittgenstein's emphasis on directly exhibited resemblances at the expense of questions of function, asking: 'How is the theory to distinguish between patience games and fortune-telling?' His answer – that we need to stress 'biological relations between the members' (relations of influence or imitation or of inherited codes) (Fowler 1982: 42) – perhaps indicates how deeply rooted the bio-logical model remains in our thinking about cultural taxonomy.

A refinement of the theory of family resemblances is the account developed in cognitive psychology of classification by prototype: the pos-tulate that we understand categories (such as *bird*) through a very con-crete logic of typicality. We take a robin or a sparrow to be more central to that category than an ostrich, and a kitchen chair to be more typical of the class of chairs than a throne or a piano stool. Rather than having clear boundaries, essential components, and shared and uniform properties, classes defined by prototypes have a common core and then fade into fuzziness at the edges (Paltridge 1997: 53). This is to say that we classify easily at the level of prototypes, and with more difficulty – extending features of the prototype by metaphor and analogy to take account of non-typical features – as we diverge from them. The *Iliad*, the *Odyssey* and the *Epic of Gilgamesh* are all texts that we class as epics, but the *Iliad* is the prototype we use to determine the category into which the others fall – and, using another prototype, we might well class the *Epic of Gilgamesh* with religious narratives such as the biblical *Genesis*. The judgement we make ('is it like this, or is it more like that?') is as much pragmatic as it is conceptual, a matter of how we wish to contextualise these texts and the uses we wish to make of them.

Bowker and Star invoke the model of categorisation by prototype in order to make a more general point about classification: that we tend

to work from what we know best in a sort of concrete and *ad hoc* negotiation of unfamiliar experiences, rather than employing a formal grid
which can be applied indifferently to any set of materials. It is not that
formal categories have no place, but rather that 'people juggle vernacular (or folk) classifications together with the most formal category
schemes', and that 'they subvert the formal schemes with informal
work-arounds' (Bowker and Star 1999: 54). A more radical conclusion
that we might draw from this discussion is that, in dealing with questions of genre, our concern should not be with matters of taxonomic
substance ('What classes and sub-classes are there? To which class does
this text belong?') – to which there are never any 'correct' answers – but
rather with questions of use: 'What models of classification are there,
and how have people made use of them in particular circumstances?' My
interest is primarily in the 'ordinary' uses of these models; but I assume
that our everyday taxonomies are to a large extent informed by the
traces of formal models, and in the rest of this chapter I therefore examine some of the central traditions of Western literary genre theory which
have so thoroughly seeped into our cultural classification systems.

PRESENTATIONAL MODES: PLATO AND ARISTOTLE

Our starting point is the third book of Plato's *Republic*, and the context
is inauspicious: Socrates is demonstrating to an acquiescent Adimantus
and his companions that verbal art must have a moral function, and that
the forms of imitation common to it are potentially corrupting of
the warrior virtues that will be found in his ideal republic. Its faults are
both of content (*logos*) and form (*lexis*), but the passages of relevance to
us have to do with the latter. Everything that is said by poets and story-
tellers, says Socrates, is 'a narration [*diêgêsis*] of past, present, or future
things', and it proceeds 'either by pure narration [*haplêi diêgêsei*] or by a
narrative that is effected through imitation [*dia mimêseôs*], or by both'
(Plato 1961: 392d). The distinction being made here is between the
speech of the poet and the represented speech of characters; in the third,
'mixed' mode, which is that of the Homeric epics for example, there is
one level of speech that tells a story, and another level of embedded
speech which is that of the characters represented at the first level.
Either the poet speaks in his own voice, or he speaks 'as if he were

someone else' (Plato 1961: 393c) – and this possibility of miming the voice and the characteristics of another person is at the heart of what troubles Socrates about poetry and drama.

The crucial move, the one that lays the basis for Western genre theory, then takes place with the identification of these three modes of representation of speech with particular genres. Socrates summarises as follows:

> Now I think I can make plain to you what I was unable to before, that there is one kind of poetry and taletelling which works wholly through imitation, as you remarked, tragedy and comedy, and another which employs the recital of the poet himself, best exemplified, I presume, in the dithyramb, and there is again that which employs both, in epic poetry and in many other places, if you apprehend me.

> (Plato 1961: 394c)

Of the many problems raised by this passage, let me single out only the one which is presented by the mention of the **dithyramb**: a sort of choric hymn to the god Dionysus, the few extant fragments of which hardly seem to be examples of 'pure narration', yet which are certainly not lyric poems in the modern sense of the word. The dichotomy through which Socrates organises this trilogy of genres (**figural** imitation / authorial narration) thus bears an ambiguous relation to the later generic triads that have been derived from it and which tend to designate the lyric as their third category. It is in any case clear that there is no systematic articulation of the poetic genres here, but only a set of generic examples drawn from an underlying distinction between two ways of representing events and characters in time.

Let us now turn to the other major theorisation of genre in antiquity, Aristotle's *Poetics*, which begins with Aristotle saying that he will speak not only of poetry in general 'but also of its species and their respective capacities'. All of the poetic kinds, he writes, are 'modes of imitation', but they differ from one another in three respects: 'either by a difference of kind in their means, or by differences in the objects, or in the manner of their imitations'.

The *means* of imitation can be such things as colour and form, or the human voice; but in the case of verbal art the means are 'rhythm, language [*logôi*], and harmony', in varying combinations (Aristotle 1941: 1447a). The *object* of imitation (the subject matter of poetry) is human action [*praxis*], performed by agents who are either good or bad, and who can thus be classed as superior, inferior, or equal to us. Finally, the genres of poetry differ by *manner*. Aristotle's distinctions repeat those of Socrates:

> Given both the same means and the same kind of object for imita-
> tion, one may either (1) speak at one moment in narrative and at
> another in an assumed character, as Homer does; or (2) one may
> remain the same throughout, without any such change; or (3) the imi-
> tators may represent the whole story dramatically, as though they
> were actually doing the things described.
>
> (Aristotle 1941: 1448a)

Now, the specification of different objects of imitation – essentially a theory of **decorum**, the stylistic level that is appropriate to different spheres of action – does potentially lead towards a genuine theorisation of genre, and Aristotle uses it as the basis of his distinction between comedy and tragedy. But by 'means' Aristotle understands something like the **semiotic medium** in which a text is embedded, involving colour and line, three-dimensional mass, the tone and pitch of the human voice, projected light ...; and by 'manner' he understands the presentational modes which differentiate narrative from dramatic storytelling. As Gérard Genette argues, the fact that the *Poetics* deals only with tragedy and the epic means that Plato's distinction between pure and impure narrative categories drops out, replaced by a single category of narrative exemplified by the epic, not the dithyramb – the latter, he argues, is a kind of 'phantom genre' since all narrative is more or less 'impure', i.e., has dramatic elements (Genette 1992: 21–2).

The world of verbal art is thus divided between two major presentational modes: authorial speech which tells us about human actions, and the speech of characters who act. One way of expressing this would be as an opposition between monologue and dialogue; but this doesn't really go to the heart of things, because, as we have already seen, (monologic) narrative can always include other voices within it, and in any case, as Bakhtin would argue, any monologue is always ultimately a dialogue in so far as it anticipates a potential audience. Another way of putting it would be in terms of Henry James's opposition between (narrative) 'telling' and (dramatic) 'showing'; but this misses the verbal dimension that both presentational modes have in common. Perhaps the clearest way of expressing the opposition between these two categories is through the Bakhtinian dichotomy of the representational and the represented word: language that refers both to the world and to other language, and language embedded *within* other language. While this still leaves open the question of the peculiar semiotic status of drama as a story without a teller, and indeed is reductive in thinking of drama – as Plato does – as 'mixed' speech with the narrative connections subtracted, it does get at some of the complexities of the layering of one piece of speech within another, the tension between voices in any **poetics** of quotation; and it thus opens up the question of the relation between language, voice, and voiced bodies. The exemplary question posed by Roland Barthes in *S/Z*, 'Qui parle?', 'Who is it that is speaking here?', is still the most difficult and the most interesting of textual questions (Barthes 1990: 41).

THE NATURAL FORMS

These are not, however, the questions that have dominated Western genre theory over the last 2400 years. Rather, it has taken one of two pathways: on the one hand, it has contented itself with a listing of the empirically existing genres, without concern for the grounds on which they are differentiated; on the other, it has attempted to develop a systematic account of genre on the basis of a misreading of the Socratic triad.

The first of these traditions is at once the more prevalent and the less interesting. The great Roman rhetorician Quintilian recommends a number of genres to those who would become orators: history, philosophy, three classes of oratory, and eight poetic genres – epic (which includes didactic, pastoral, and scientific works such as those of Hesiod, Theocritus, and Lucretius), tragedy, **Old Comedy**, **New Comedy**, elegy, iambic (poetry in iambic metre), satire, and lyric poetry. Some of these seem to be defined by their metrical form, some by their mode of presentation, and some by their content or their characteristic attitude towards the world. Much the same list can be found in Sidney's *Defence of Poesie*, written in 1580–1, and in the *artes poeticae* (arts of poetry, or poetics) of many other Renaissance authors. The emergence of new genres such as tragicomedy does little to disturb the dominant paradigm, in which an Aristotelian schema concerned with the epic and the dramatic coexists with an empirical and descriptive account of those genres Aristotle doesn't mention. Thus Boileau's *Art poétique* (1674) deals in canto 3 with the major genres of epic, tragedy, and comedy, while canto 2 'strings together idyll, elegy, ode, sonnet, epigram, rondeau, madrigal, ballad, satire, vaudeville, and song, without any comprehensive classification'; and Rapin's *Réflexions sur la poétique* of the same year argues that, while nearly all genres can be reduced to epic (narration) and drama (action), all those that cannot are to be considered 'imperfect' (Genette 1992: 26–7).

The second tradition of systematic theorisation of genre involves the attribution to Aristotle of a division of the universe of literary genres into the *epic* (or narrative), the *dramatic*, and the *lyric*, and this tradition has been the subject of an important revisionist essay by the French critic Gérard Genette, *The Architext*, originally published in 1979 and which I follow closely in the next few pages. It is lyric poetry that is the problematic term in this triad. Aristotle is silent about it, apart from brief references to the flute and the lyre, and Plato's use of the dithyramb to exemplify pure narrative (*diêgêsis*, which can perhaps also be translated as 'presentation') has been the opposite of clarifying. The problem is simply that 'lyric', which comes to occupy the slot for which dithyramb is the example, is not a narrative genre, and it is not clear that it is a fundamental mode of presentation of speech at all. The move that is tentatively made by the Hellenistic critics is to transform the three *modes of presentation of speech* (authorial, figural, and mixed) into three *genres*; this is the term (*genera*) used by Diomedes in the late fourth century. From the late Renaissance – Irene Behrens notes its occurrence in Minturno's essay *De Poeta* (1559), and there are later references in Cervantes, Milton, and Dryden – the third 'genre' is designated as the lyric, and the now-familiar triad of the epic, dramatic, and lyrical starts to become conventional currency.

The attraction of this schema is clear: it is comprehensive, covering the major areas of imaginative writing, although on closer examination it turns out that there are some important exclusions; it allows for an exhaustive differentiation of these areas; and it allows for conceptually elegant philosophising about the relations between writing and human experience. When Friedrich Schlegel complained in 1797 that 'We already have so many theories about poetic genres. Why have we no concept of poetic genre?' (Schlegel 1957), it was to this lack of what David Duff calls 'a *philosophical* theory of genre, as distinct from a purely descriptive account of individual genres' (Duff 2000: 3), that he was calling attention. Yet these three forms, which are adjectival in nature rather than nominal – the epical, the dramatic, the lyrical – are larger than the individual genres, which they contain. Goethe thus distinguishes, in two of the notes appended in 1819 to the *West-östlicher Divan*, between the multiplicity of genres proper or *Dichtarten* (allegory, ballad, drama, elegy, epistle, fable, idyll, ode, novel, parody, romance, satire ...), with their heterogeneous criteria, and the three 'natural forms', the *drei echte Naturformen der Dichtung*: the epic mode of lucid and detached narration, the lyric mode of enthusiastic excitement, and the dramatic mode of personal action (Goethe 1966: 480). The latter are essential, 'inner forms' rather than contingent and historically variable ways of writing, and they divide the universe of writing between three different sets of expressive and conceptual capacities.

This way of thinking about writing gives rise to an extensive speculative activity that seeks to theorise the fields of sense that it takes the 'natural forms' to be. For Hegel, the epic mode is the vehicle of an objective disclosure of the exterior universe, and it corresponds to the childhood of the human race; lyric is the subjective disclosure of the inner world of particularised individuals, and it has to do with the separation of the personal self from the community; and drama is the synthesis of the two, the objectification of subjectivities in dialogue and action. For other writers each mode is associated with a different tense, a different grammatical person (first-person lyric, second-person drama, third-person epic), a different psychological set. For Karl Viëtor the modes convey three 'basic attitudes', with the lyric expressing feeling, the epic, knowledge, and drama, the will; for Ernest Bovet they are 'essential modes of conceiving life and the universe' (Hernardi 1972: 12, 17).

One of the most lucid summaries of this whole tradition of seeing the three 'natural' forms as possessing essential qualities is given in the aesthetic speculations of the young Stephen Dedalus in James Joyce's *A Portrait of the Artist as a Young Man* (1916):

> Art necessarily divides itself into three forms progressing from one to the next. These forms are: the lyrical form, the form wherein the artist presents his image in immediate relation to himself; the epical form wherein he presents his image in mediate relation to himself and to others; the dramatic form, the form wherein he presents his image in immediate relation to others.

Stephen then goes on to enumerate the expressive qualities of each of these forms:

> The lyrical form is in fact the simplest verbal vesture of an instant of emotion, a rhythmical cry such as ages ago cheered on the man who pulled at the oar or dragged stones up a slope. He who utters it is more conscious of the instant of emotion than of himself as feeling emotion. The simplest epical form is seen emerging out of lyrical literature when the artist prolongs and broods upon himself as the centre of an epical event and this form progresses till the centre of emotional gravity is equidistant from the artist himself and from others. The narrative is no longer purely personal. The personality of the artist passes into the narration itself. ... The dramatic form is reached when the vitality which has flowed and eddied round each person fills every person with such vital force that he or she assumes a proper and intangible aesthetic life. The personality of the artist, at first a cry or cadence or a mood and then a fluid and lambent narrative, finally refines itself out of existence, impersonalises itself, so to speak ...
>
> (Joyce 1960: 213–15)

The 'progress[ion] from one to the next' is a theory at once of psychological stages and of historical development, the one mapped onto the other. Victor Hugo sketches out a similar evolutionary schema in the preface to his play *Cromwell* (1827), and indeed it was to become a nineteenth-century commonplace. The three forms, that is to say, are capable of organising infinitely expanding fields of significance which are mapped onto each other with little restriction in terms of their analytic relevance. They become a 'taxonomic kaleidoscope in which the too-seductive pattern of the triad – a form receptive to any meaning at all – passes through endless metamorphoses, surviving on the crest of dubious reckonings ... and interchangeable attributions' (Genette 1992: 44).

An important qualification to this essentialist view of the three spheres of generic sense is made when Goethe's two distinct categories of genres (*Dichtarten*) and the natural forms (*Dichtweisen*, or *Naturformen*) are taken to hold a more complex relation to each other. Thus Emil Staiger (1991) conceives the three *Naturformen* as *styles* rather than as genres, which means that a drama may, for example, be 'lyrical' in its expressive key (*Tonart*). This move, which distinguishes between the 'stylistic' and 'generic' dimensions of 'lyric', 'epic', and 'drama', generates a tension between the natural kinds and genres proper and thus a much wider range of possible combinations. One way of formalising this dual set of variables is through the figure, proposed by Goethe and carried to parodic extremes by Julius Petersen, of a wheel in which the three spokes represent the natural kinds, and specific genres are distributed around the wheel in relative proximity to or distance from them. Alternatively, more subtle differentiation can be achieved by sub-dividing the generic triad into further triads. Albert Guérard thus proposes the following classification:

> Lyrical lyric: Goethe's 'Wanderers Nachtlied'
> Epic (narrative) lyric: 'Ballad of Sir Patrick Spens'
> Dramatic lyric: Browning's dramatic monologues
>
> Lyrical epic: Byron's *Don Juan*
> Epic narrative: *Iliad*
> Dramatic epic: *A Tale of Two Cities*
>
> Lyrical drama: *The Tempest*
> Epic drama: Shelley's *Prometheus Unbound*, the plays of Aeschylus
> Dramatic drama: the plays of Molière
>
> (Guérard 1940: 197ff)

All such schemata, however, continue to beg the question of the logical relation between the three natural kinds: that is, the question of whether they can be distinguished exhaustively from each other by means of criteria which are the same for each. The Socratic triad of sub-genres, and that by working from the general to the particular we can understand something of the complementary structures of truth, temporality, and subjectivity that flow down to inform the individual genres. The logical relationship is something like that between genus and species, a metonymic relation of the part to the whole.

Yet these wholes are no longer, as they were for Plato and Aristotle, merely enunciative structures (the forms of representation of speech), since they have a thematic dimension: the natural forms are expressive of states of mind, or of attitudes towards the world, or of temporal patternings. Genette thus views them as a something like *archigenres*:

> Archi-, because each of them is supposed to overarch and include, ranked by degree of importance, a certain number of empirical genres that – whatever their amplitude, longevity, or potential for recurrence – are apparently phenomena of culture and history; but still (or already) – genres, because ... their defining criteria always involve a thematic element that eludes purely formal or linguistic description.
>
> (Genette 1992: 64–5)

Underlying this judgement is a prior theoretical distinction between *genres*, which Genette takes to be defined by their thematic content and to be 'properly literary categories' (Genette 1992: 64), and the enunciative *modes* specified by Plato and Aristotle, defined by their different forms of presentation of speech and belonging to that branch of linguistics called *pragmatics* which is concerned with the actions effected by texts. Northrop Frye, as Genette notes, is one of the few modern critics to have developed this conception of the pragmatic underpinnings of literary speech, writing that 'words may be acted in front of a spectator; they may be spoken in front of a listener; they may be sung or chanted; or they may be written for a reader' (Frye 1967: 247). Claudio Guillén likewise suggests that there are more than three pragmatic modes: together with 'storytelling, rhythmic song, and dramatic simulation' he cites 'monologic discourse' and letter-writing (Guillén 1986: 81). Frye calls this dimension of literary language the 'radical of presentation'; it could also be thought of as an aspect of the semiotic medium in which texts are embedded.

authorial, figural, and mixed speech does indeed use a simple and un
sal logical distinction, that between narration and dramatic imitat
diêgêsis and *mimesis*, as its basis; but these can be treated on the s
plane only in so far as drama is thought of as a sort of *failed* narration
Socrates, dramatic imitation occurs 'when one removes the words of
poet between and leaves the alternating speeches' (Plato 1961: 394b)
formal definition is as narration *plus* imitated speech *minus* narration.

In Joyce, similarly, the criterion of the immediate or mediated relat
of self to other generates ambiguities for each of the three forms. W
would the 'immediate relation to others' of drama actually mean, since
this schema there are actually two different kinds of others: they are
tively represented in the epic but are the embodied and self-represent
sources of speech in drama. And does not this placing of self and oth
on the same plane blur important distinctions between the author,
position of enunciation, and fictional characters? In what sense is ly
poetry an 'immediate relation to the self'? Is it merely epic speech with
the characters, and might the lyric 'I' not be considered a form of charac
a figuring-forth rather than a direct expression of the self? And how wou
the difference between first-person and third-person narration affect t
proposed 'mediate relation' between the artist and his characters?

Finally, the schema of the natural forms poses difficult questio
both of exclusion and of inclusion. To which mode are we to assi
'the essay, the feuilleton, the puzzle, the formal address, the newspap
report, the polemical satire, and the proverb' (Hernardi 1972: 34–5
On the other hand, the essentialist logic of the schema leads to an ov
inclusiveness which means that difficult or 'intellectual' poets such
Góngora, Hölderlin, Mallarmé, or Prynne are assimilated to the 'rhyt
mical cry' of the lyric, or that the ascription of the novel to the 'ep
mode leads the Hungarian critic Georg Lukács to think of the lat
genre as a 'degraded epic'. Whenever particular, historically continge
genres are subsumed within these larger patterns, the problems of log
cal fit become formidable.

GENRES AND MODES

The assumption is always that, whatever the tensions between them
these larger forms govern and define the more specific genres an

The problem with the Romantic triad, and with its fallacious geneal-ogy, is that it confuses these two different orders of organisation: the logical order of the Platonic and Aristotelian 'modes' (' "there are and there can only be three ways of representing actions in language," etc.') with the his-torical and thematic order of genres (' "there are and there can only be three basic poetic outlooks," etc.') (Genette 1992: 70). Presentational modes are, for Genette, something like *a priori* forms of literary expression, whereas genres are historically contingent and variable. And because these are dis-tinct orders, they cannot be thought to be in a relation of inclusion. Whilst any genre (the novel, say) can subsume smaller sets within it (sub-genres such as the novel of manners or ideas, the detective novel, the picaresque, or the historical novel), there can be no such hierarchical relation between modes and genres, since 'mode neither includes nor implies theme; theme neither includes nor implies mode' (Genette 1992: 73).

What I would now like to suggest is that the term 'mode' be reserved for use in a somewhat different sense. (One of the inherent problems with working with genre theory is of course the lack of an agreed and coherent terminology.) What I mean by this is the 'adjecti-val' sense suggested by Fowler, in which modes are understood as the extensions of certain genres beyond specific and time-bound formal structures to a broader specification of 'tone'. Genette speaks of an exis-tential or anthropological 'feeling' 'that is properly epical, lyrical, dra-matic – but also tragic, comic, elegiac, fantastic, romantic, etc.' (Genette 1992: 67). Rather than standing alone, modes are usually qualifications or modifications of particular genres (*gothic* thriller, *pastoral* elegy, *satirical* sitcom), and in this respect they resemble the first term in Guérard's classificatory scheme (*dramatic* lyric, *lyrical* drama, *epic* drama ...); they specify thematic features and certain forms and modali-ties of speech, but not the formal structures or even the semiotic medium through which the text is to be realised.

A modal term thus suggests 'that some of the nonstructural fea-tures of a kind are extended to modify another kind': if we call *Emma* a comic novel, 'we mean that *Emma* is by kind a novel, by mode comic' (Fowler 1982: 107, 106). The modes start their life as genres but over time take on a more general force which is detached from particular structural embodiments: tragedy moves from designating only a dra-matic form and comes to refer to the sense of the tragic in any medium whatsoever; pastoral modulates from the georgic or the eclogue into a broader form which can be applied to any genre that deals with an idealised countryside populated by simple folk. Exhausted genres such as the Gothic romance may survive in their modal form – quite spectacularly so in the case of the gothic mode, which passes through early-Victorian stage melodrama into the stories of Edgar Allan Poe and the novels of Charles Dickens, and thence into the vampire novel, the detective novel, and a number of other narrative genres, and more directly from melodrama into a range of Hollywood genres including the 'old house' movie, *film noir*, and the contemporary horror movie. Equally, modes, like genres, may themselves become exhausted: Fowler cites the heroic mode as one that has largely become obsolete (Fowler 1982: 111).

The concept of mode would include, but is not limited to, such forms as the heroic, the tragic, the comic, the lyrical, the picaresque, the elegiac, the encyclopaedic, the satiric, the romance, the fantastic, the pastoral, the epigrammatic, the didactic, and the melodramatic. It corresponds in part to Frye's four basic 'plots' – the tragic, the comic, the romantic, and the satiric/ironic – rather than to what he calls modes (Frye 1967: 162); and the Romantic triad of epic, dramatic, and lyric are perhaps properly thought of as modes in the 'adjectival' sense in which I am using it. Barbara Lewalski notes that Sidney's eight major 'parts, kinds or species' of poetry – '*Heroick, Lyrick, Tragick, Comick, Satyrick, Iambick, Elegiack, Pastorall*, and certaine others' – are all described by modal qualities of tone rather than being understood as genres (Lewalski 1986: 6). Claudio Guillén describes the epistolary form in such a way that it seems to work at once as a radical of presentation (a structure of address), as a genre (the letter), and as a mode characterised by such 'tonal' features as 'the sense of place and time, the ability to imagine the other, the willingness to let the words affect the words, process and improvisation as a form' (Guillén 1986: 83). When William Empson (1966) considers 'proletarian literature', John Gay's *The Beggar's Opera* (1728), and Lewis Carroll's *Alice* books (1865 and 1872) as forms of pastoral, he is writing about the pastoral mode, not about the more specific pastoral genre. Angus Fletcher says that allegory 'is properly considered a mode' since 'it is a fundamental process of encoding our speech' (Fletcher 1964: 3). And Michael Holquist argues that Mikhail

Bakhtin uses the term 'novel' in a consistently modal rather than a generic sense:

> 'Novel' is the name Bakhtin gives to whatever force is at work within a given literary system to reveal the limits, the artificial constraints of that system. ... What is more conventionally thought of as the novel is simply the most complex and distilled expression of this impulse. ... Even the drama (Ibsen and the other Naturalists), the long poem (*Childe Harold* or *Don Juan*) or the lyric (as in Heine) become masks for the novel during the nineteenth century. As formerly distinct literary genres are subjected to the novel's intensifying antigeneric power, their systematic purity is infected and they become 'novelised'.
>
> (Holquist 1981: xxxi–xxxii)

In the terminology that I use in this book, then, I distinguish between the following forms of organisation of texts, whether verbal, aural or visual:

- the *semiotic medium* in which a text is inscribed and presented (speech or writing, colour and line, three-dimensional mass, the tone and pitch of the human voice or of other sounds, recorded and projected light ...);
- the *'radical of presentation'* through which the text is presented to its receiver (first- or third-person narration, dramatic narration, non-narrative address, song, and so on);
- *mode* in the adjectival sense as a thematic and tonal qualification or 'colouring' of genre;
- *genre* or kind, a more specific organisation of texts with thematic, rhetorical and formal dimensions; and
- *sub-genre*, the further specification of genre by a particular thematic content.

Apart from the relation between genre and sub-genre, these forms of textual organisation should not be thought to be hierarchically ordered between themselves. They are discontinuous with one another, and they imply no derivation of one order of form from another.

POETICS AND HISTORY

Yet still none of this solves the problem of how to describe the logic of
genre, the logic of the shifting mass of really-existing historical genres
that Goethe characterised as 'external contingent forms' (Goethe 1966:
482). I mean 'describe' in two different but related senses. First, there is
the question of the order formed between and among genres: is it possible to differentiate exhaustively between genres using a small number of
consistent criteria? Or should the order of genres rather be thought of as
a shifting historical system made up of heterogeneous entities? Second,
there is the question of the logical order of which any particular genre is
composed: a logic at once of its 'internal' structure and of its strategic
relation to a 'recurrent situation'.

These two sets of questions cannot, however, be considered in isolation from each other. The 'internal' order of a genre, its particular configuration of form and function, cannot be separated from its relation to
other genres. Here I draw on two principles enunciated in the later
writings of the **Russian Formalists** (I discuss these at greater length in
Frow 1986: 83–102). The first is that genres form a constantly shifting
hierarchical order within certain limited domains. This is true of the literary field because of its **overdetermination** by social values and social
conflicts, and *a priori* of every other field of institutionalised discursive
value; it is probably less true, however, of 'informal' domains such as
everyday talk, technical talk, or domains of minimal social esteem such
as the riddle. It follows from this, second, that all genres within a particular field are interrelated, and shifts in the 'internal' structure of genres, their constant modification as new instances transform the genre,
interact with the order formed by the generic field.

Genre is thus the driving force of change in the literary field. It is, as
Todorov puts it, 'the meeting place between general poetics and event-
based literary history' (Todorov 1990: 19–20): between a systematic
account of structures and an account of historical change. An adequate
description of genre will involve a fusion of these two perspectives. It
will look something like a historical poetics, in which the structural
components of genre are taken to be historically specific rather than
obeying a purely formal logic.

It will thus not repeat the urge towards systemic inclusiveness that
characterised much of nineteenth-century poetics in its embrace of the

theory of the three natural forms; it will not look for a 'natural' order but for orders of relation which are social and historical. By the same token it will avoid the systems-building of early structuralist theory, which worked by means of the construction of a calculus of all of the possible combinations of generic relations, features, and themes. What this combinatory table is supposed to yield is a set of abstract types, of 'theoretical' genres which, in terms that precisely repeat Goethe's opposition of an 'inner necessity' to 'external contingent forms' (Goethe 1966: 482), correspond to a structural logic rather than to the surface manifestations of this logic in the disorderly array of 'historical' genres (Todorov 1975: 17–21). The theoretical genres will 'sometimes correspond to existing genres, sometimes to models of writing that have functioned at different periods; at still other times they do not correspond to anything – they are like an empty square in the Mendeleevian system that could only be filled by a literature to come' (Ducrot and Todorov 1981: 150): a structuralist science of genre would allow the theorist to predict the place that will be occupied by genres that as yet have no existence.

Tzvetan Todorov has been the major exponent of this fantasy of a rigorously systemic approach to genre, one that is modelled on Vladimir Propp's analysis of folkloric tales in terms of a range of possible combinations of a small number of basic motifs, and his later work mercifully abandons it. In *Genres in Discourse* he writes that genres are 'only the classes of texts that have been historically perceived as such': historical rather than theoretical entities. They are not, however, merely metadiscursive entities – not just arbitrary names – since they have properties that can be described. The mode of existence of genres is social: 'In a given society the recurrence of certain discursive properties is institutionalised, and individual texts are produced and perceived in relation to the norm constituted by that codification. A genre, whether literary or not, is nothing other than the codification of discursive properties' (Todorov 1990: 17–18). It is because they have this institutional existence that they can work as a '**horizon of expectation**' for readers and as 'models of writing' for authors: 'On the one hand, authors write in function of (which does not mean in agreement with) the existing generic system. ... On the other hand, readers read in function of the generic system, with which they are familiar thanks to criticism, schools, the book distribution system, or simply by hearsay' (Todorov 1990: 18–19).

But does this move merely return us to that 'empirical' tradition of literary analysis that so signally failed to develop an adequate theorisation of genre? Isn't there a danger that this move from 'theoretical' to 'historical' genres, seen as a historically specific codification of particular clusters of discursive properties, could entail a return to the mere descriptive listing of all the genres that there are? This is the problem that H.R. Jauss struggles with in his important essay on the genre systems of the European Middle Ages, 'Theory of Genres and Medieval Literature'.

Literary genre theory, he writes, seeks a path between 'the Scylla of nominalist scepticism that allows for only aposteriori classifications' (that is, it allows one to use only the concepts that a period itself elaborates) and 'the Charybdis of regression into timeless typologies' (Jauss 1982: 78). Grasping genre in a properly historical way, apprehending them *in re*, in the process of becoming, rather than normatively (*ante rem*) or in a purely descriptive taxonomy (*post rem*), means that one should 'ascribe no other generality to literary "genres" ... than that which manifests itself in the course of its historical appearance' (Jauss 1982: 79). Genres are not logical classes but rather '*groups* or *historical families*. As such, they cannot be deduced or defined, but only historically determined, delimited, and described' (Jauss 1982: 80).

This does not mean, however, that their historicity is purely contingent. Just as genres form a **horizon of expectations** against which any text is read, so are they themselves subsumed within a broader horizon formed by a period's system of genres. Even the literature of the Middle Ages, Jauss writes, 'is no arbitrary sum of its parts, but rather a latent ordering or sequence of orderings of literary genres' (Jauss 1982: 95). These orderings form a kind of 'immanent poetics' of any period, an implicit ordering of texts and genres which can be glimpsed in such things as the principles by which anthologies are organised or by competitive references to other genres. The example Jauss gives is that of the prologue to the oldest part of the *Roman de Renart*, in which:

> the jongleur, who boasts of his object as a totally new thing, distinguishes it from a series of well-known individual works and genres: *troja* (ancient romance), *tristan* (Breton romance), fabliau, chanson

de geste, and then an unidentified animal poem. ... This list of the works that were popular around 1176/77 allows one to grasp a literary system in so far as the genres that are specified are not just accidentally selected, but rather form the specific horizon of expectations before which the new and often parodistic conte [tale] ... must take place.

(Jauss 1982: 97)

Genre systems form a shifting hierarchy, made up of tensions between 'higher' and 'lower' genres, a constant alternation of the dominant form, and a constant renewal of genres through processes of specialisation or recombination. Genres, it follows, are neither self-identical nor self-contained. The principle of thinking about them in historical and processual terms means that we must relinquish the notion of 'a constant number of unchangeable essential characteristics for the individual genres', as well as 'the correlative notion of a sequence of literary genres closed within themselves, encapsulated from one another'. Instead, we should take as our focus 'the reciprocal relations that make up the literary system of a given historical moment' (Jauss 1982: 105).

Jauss's projected 'historical systematics' seems to me to be roughly akin to what Todorov means by the notion of an institutionalised codification of the discursive properties of a genre. Together I think they spell out a kind of answer to the first of the two questions I asked about how to describe genre: that is, they suppose that the order formed between and among genres should be regarded as a historically changing system rather than as a logical order. Such an approach makes it possible to bring together the categories of a poetics with those of the historical event: if genres are actual and contingent forms rather than necessary and essential forms, they are nevertheless not arbitrary. And this in turn means that the 'internal' organisation of genre, the object of my second question, can be understood in terms of particular historical codifications of discursive properties. It is to a discussion of these structural features that I turn in the following chapter.

4

IMPLICATION AND RELEVANCE

THE STRUCTURAL DIMENSIONS OF GENRE

Let us take as our starting point the assumption that all genres possess historically specific and variable *expressive capacities*: they offer frameworks for constructing meaning and value in one or another medium. These frameworks are alternative to each other, and choices between them have to do with my valuing of certain expressive qualities over others in a particular set of circumstances: I choose to make or to watch a documentary rather than a feature film, or rather than writing or reading a newspaper article, because that genre allows me to activate certain possibilities of meaning and value rather than others.

Now, this expressive capacity can be analysed in terms of the sorts of **truth effects** generated by the discursive qualities of the genre. By 'discursive qualities' I mean the *semiotic medium*, with the structures of authorship and reception that tend to accompany it in certain kinds of setting, and the particular *strategies* that tend to organise the documentary film (for example). These include a set of *formal features*: a historically variable repertoire that might include the use of voice-over, of interviews with informants, of black-and-white film stock, of hand-held cameras, of certain rhythms of editing, and so on; the *thematic structures* usually associated with the genre, the *topoi* of 'public affairs', in a very general sense, usually mediated through the perspective of participants; and a certain *structure of address*: a set of assumptions about who (that is, what kind of person) is speaking, and with what authority and credibility, to whom. As Ann Imbrie expresses these distinctions, genre is defined 'by the way it expresses human experience (subject matter) through an identifiable form (formal character) that clarifies or discovers the values in or attitude toward that experience (generic attitude)' (Imbrie 1986: 60).

Let me now try to put this into a more schematic form. I understand genre to be a historically specific pattern of organisation of semiotic material along a number of dimensions in a specific medium and in relation to particular types of situational constraints which help shape this pattern. Genre in turn acts as a constraint upon – that is, a structuring and shaping of – meaning and value at the level of text for certain strategic ends; it produces effects of truth and authority that are specific to it, and projects a 'world' that is generically specific.

The *semiotic medium* and *physical setting* constitute a material and technical matrix within which genres are embedded. They are not themselves a component of genre, but they form part of the framing conditions which govern and may signal generic structure, and they have direct consequences for the structural organisation of genre. For the street poster bearing a news headline, the wooden hoarding and its physical proximity to a newsagent's shop constitute the poster as a display and have immediate effects upon the organisation of that display: bold and large typeface, the sense of the message's urgency, the effect of 'hailing' the passer-by, and so on. For the documentary, the medium of film involves not only the film stock but also the optical capacities of cameras and editing suites, the apparatus of sound recording, the set-up of a studio, the costs of production, and the possible screening outlets. All of these inform and constrain the representational possibilities available to the film-maker, and thus the ways in which he or she can address a viewer. For the riddle, finally, the semiotic medium is either the human voice or print: we might wish to say that two different genres correspond to these media, or we might say that an original and constitutive orality is reproduced in the print medium, or that the print riddle may even become autonomous of its oral beginnings. In either case, orality or its traces strongly inform the question-and-answer structure of the riddle.

The structural dimensions that cluster together to constitute the specific configuration of a genre can be expressed in a variety of ways, but for the sake of simplicity I describe them as follows:

1   The *formal organisation* of a genre comprises the repertoire of ways of shaping the material medium in which it works and the 'immaterial' categories of time, space, and enunciative position. The shaping of the medium might involve, for example, the organisation of the material properties of language (sound patterns, rhythm, pitch), of the layout of printed pages, or of the properties of grammar and syntax (for example, the degree of complexity of sentences, and the way they play off against metrical units). It involves such basic choices as whether texts in the genre are normally long or short, spoken or written, in verse or prose, and it stipulates certain kinds of textual cohesion – as we saw in the use of the question-and-answer format in the riddle, for example. There are corresponding choices for other representational media: for paintings they might involve ways of organising the texture of paint, the relations of mass to colour and to line, and the relation of the painting's lines of force to each other and to the frame. At the level of story and character, formal organisation involves the shaping of the temporal and spatial relations of the projected world, the quality and duration of actions, and the relation between the central narrative 'voice' or perspective and the figure of the author, on the one hand, and the represented world on the other, which in turn sets up a certain temporal relation between the present of narration and the narrated time. This enunciative structure also specifies certain kinds of tone and certain effects of verisimilitude: the presentation of the text is in a 'literal' or a **'figurative'** mode, its manner is elevated or modest or somewhere in between, and a certain kind of subject matter corresponds to these stylistic choices. The *sermo humilis*, or 'low style', of the New Testament, for example, produces effects of everydayness which are quite different from the elevated tone of some of the prophetic books of the Old Testament, and thereby mark a theological shift which has been of major historical consequence.

2   The *rhetorical structure* of a genre has to do with the way textual relations between the senders and receivers of messages are organised in a structured situation of address. This structure may be either

immediate, as when two speakers are present to each other and speaking in their 'own' voice, or mediated by more or less complex projections of voices or perspectives from actual or implied speakers. At the most general level, the speech situation organises relations of power and solidarity between speakers (or their textual representatives), and organises the kinds of semantic intention they bring to it. To speak is to make statements which are not only declarative but evaluative: my words express not only a state of affairs in the world but an indication of the degree of my commitment to its obligatoriness, desirability, likelihood, or reality. This is the logic of what linguists call *modality*, the expression of the necessity or possibility of a state of affairs, of my knowledge or belief about it, of obligation, permission, desire or preference in relation to it, and of the timescale in which I say that it is located. Relations between speakers thus involve a negotiation and an agreement (or disagreement) about the kind of truth status that is to be attributed to what is being talked about: it may be fictitious or non-fictitious, a matter of opinion or absolute truth, a truth of this world or of some other; it is 'keyed' and qualified in particular ways. Credibility, authority, and emotional tone are effects of these rhetorical relations and of their formal expression in the syntactic and intonational nuances of discourse (or the corresponding forms of modal nuancing available in other media: photographic realism or impressionist suggestion in nineteenth-century painting, for example). The degree of formality of an utterance (its decorum) is another of the ways in which both a relationship between speaker and hearer and a set of implications about what kind of world is being projected from it are conveyed.

3   The *thematic content* of a genre can be thought of as the shaped human experience that a genre invests with significance and interest. In formal terms this shaping is expressed as a set of *topoi*, recurrent topics of discourse, or as a recurrent **iconography**, or as recurrent forms of argumentation. In music we might say that it is expressed as the emotional tone characteristically carried by musical forms: quietly meditative in the nocturne or the evening raga, plaintive in the country-and-western ballad, triumphant in the military march, drivingly energetic in techno. ... In those genres of

discourse that tell stories set within a recognisable world, the thematic content will be kinds of action, the kinds of actors who perform them, and the significance that accrues to actions and actors. Actions will be of different kinds: they may be world-historical occurrences, or sustained adventures, or one-off events; they will have different sorts of duration and intensity; and actors will be recognisable characters, human or non-human, belonging to the genre's more or less limited repertoire of character-types. Together, actions and actors form a world with a particular organisation of space and time and a particular mode and degree of plausibility: it will be symbolic, or exemplary, or empirically factual, and it will be presented as historically true, or as possible, or as probable (cf. Jauss 1982: 83–7). Represented worlds are always, and by definition, generically specific.

The point of this analysis is that genres are always complex structures which must be defined in terms of all three of these dimensions: the formal, the rhetorical, and the thematic. But I want to add two brief codas to this analysis.

The first is that, as will be clear, there is considerable overlap between these three dimensions; they are not neatly separate, but could each be expressed in terms of one of the other categories. Thus in an important sense each of these three dimensions is 'formal', since they involve recurrent structures: the configuration of the situation of enunciation is as much a matter of formal patterning as of rhetorical address; stylistic decorum is a matter of 'style', of address, and of a particular kind of content. Similarly, each of these dimensions is 'rhetorical' in the sense that each of them has to do with shaping and invoking the kind and quality of attention to the text that the genre prescribes: thematic material must 'interest' the receiver, and the text's formal framework deploys patterning as part of its powers of persuasion in its stance towards the other. Finally, each of these dimensions can be thought to be 'thematic' in the sense that *formal and rhetorical structures always convey meaning*: an understanding of this is central to my argument about genre.

The second coda has to do with the unequal relations between the three dimensions of genre. If I were to describe the structure of a sonnet or of a haiku, formal considerations would occupy the foreground of my description, although I would also have to talk about the structure of address and the thematic field that is prescribed – differently at different periods – for each genre. The Latin elegy of Propertius or Tibullus is similarly characterised primarily by its formal features, notably the metrical structure of the elegiac couplet; but more modern forms of the elegy have no necessary formal structure other than that of verse, whereas they do have a more strictly defined thematic content, mourning for the dead. Letters or weblogs or aphorisms have much to do with the structure of address, and are less tightly constrained in terms of content. This is merely to say that different genres give a different weight to the formal, rhetorical, or thematic dimensions of their structure, and have a characteristic constellation in each of the three areas. But it is nevertheless central to my definition of genre that each of these three dimensions has a constitutive role, and that there is no genre whose properties are not codified in each of them. It is this that allows us to distinguish genre from organisations of discourse which are *more* general (for example, from mode, style, speech variety, or **discursive formation**) and *less* general (for example, speech acts).

IMPLICATION AND PRESUPPOSITION

But how are generically specific 'worlds' projected on the basis of these structural properties? That is to say, how is it that a text generates, within the constraints of a particular generic frame, a much larger structure of meaning which is not 'contained' in what that text explicitly says?

With one significant difference, this is precisely the question that is asked by one of the more influential strands of natural language philosophy, initiated by the work of Paul Grice on the theory of conversational **implicatures** and developed in the discipline of pragmatics. Grice's question distinguishes between what an utterance says (that is, its truth-conditional content: what it 'literally' means) and the meanings that it actually conveys. These 'meanings' are *implicatures*: that is, 'a proposition that is implied by the utterance of a sentence in a context even though that proposition is not a part of nor an entailment of what was actually said' (Gazdar 1979: 38). Levinson offers the following example:

1   A: Can you tell me the time?
    B: Well, the milkman has come.

A literal paraphrase of this exchange would yield only the following information:

2   A: Do you have the ability to tell me the time?
    B: (...) The milkman came at some time prior to the time of speaking.

Yet what is actually communicated to native speakers by this exchange would certainly contain a great deal more information, which is italicised in the following rewriting:

3   A: Do you have the ability to tell me the time *of the present moment, as standardly indicated on a watch, and if so please do so tell me.*
    B: *No I don't know the exact time of the present moment, but I can provide some information from which you may be able to deduce the approximate time, namely the milkman has come.*

(Levinson 1983: 97–8)

How do we get from (1) to (3)? Nothing in the semantic content of the utterances leads us directly from the one to the other. To explain this addition or expansion of information, Grice invokes the existence of certain assumptions that generate implicatures in ordinary conversation, where the word 'implicature' designates implications that are not direct logical consequences of a statement.

The most general assumption is what he calls the Cooperative Principle: a 'rough general principle' that participants in a conversation are expected to observe, which takes some such form as: 'Make your conversational contribution such as is required, at the stage at which it occurs, by the accepted purpose or direction of the talk exchange in which you are engaged' (Grice 1989: 26). The assumption, that is to say, is that people talking together bring a certain goodwill to the conversation and thus structure their talk in such a way as to make it comprehensible to the person they are talking to.

(Grice doesn't assume that this is *always* the case, of course: only that it is necessary if conversation is to work.) The general principle is then made more specific in the form of four maxims that are held generally to apply in the exchange of talk: these maxims – of quantity, quality, relation, and manner – are norms requiring participants in a conversation to speak transparently, economically, truthfully, and to the point.

One might object that no one really speaks like this: the Gricean speech situation resembles a philosopher's fantasy of rational and orderly conversation. But Grice's point is not that these norms are respected in practice but that they nevertheless shape the way talk actually happens. When they are being fully respected, conversational contributions will be literal; when they are flouted in some way, the assumption that cooperation is nevertheless still in force will continue to prevail and the hearer will draw inferences to make sense of an apparent anomaly. If someone says of another, 'he's a bright spark', and I know that (a) she is not talking about spark plugs or light bulbs, and (b) she has no respect for the intelligence of the person of whom she is speaking, I conclude, first, that the apparent lack of clarity and relevance is misleading, and she is using a metaphor which is clear and relevant once I understand it, and second, that she is speaking ironically rather than making a literally true statement. It is these inferences that Grice calls implicatures.

The upshot of this argument is that language generates more information than it directly 'contains', and this 'more' – the implied information that we add to the words we hear – is not directly entailed in or implied by the semantic content of the words. Grice's account is a description not of the kinds of background knowledge that are adduced in the interpretation of speech, but rather of the framework of expectations that allows us to arrive at it. His account suffers from a number of weaknesses, however. Let me mention two.

The first is that speech is understood here on the model of the rational exchange of information; even while the theory allows for deviation from this model, it nevertheless finds no place for other functions of language, such as – for example – the rhetorical function of negotiating a relationship. Moreover, its privileging of conversation as the prototype of verbal communication means that language is assumed to be immediate to a speaker and a hearer for whom words are merely the mask of the mental

state they express. The second weakness follows from this model of imme-
diacy: Grice's examples of utterances are almost all short sentences or
exchanges isolated from any context (cf. Malik 2002: 159). They thus
ignore what is of central interest to me here: the way in which the move
from what is said to what is implied is shaped in particular ways by the
social codes of genre. The effect of this simplification and abstraction is
that the background knowledges and assumptions brought to bear by the
hearer to make sense of what they hear are limited to certain kinds of
immediate and pragmatic information. Similar problems beset the theory
of inferential interpretation developed by Sperber and Wilson as an alternative to Grice's model. In their argument, inferences can be drawn from an
utterance by reference to a context, and context is understood as a body of
information additional to the semantic information encoded in the utterance; it is 'the set of premises used in interpreting an utterance', and is 'a
psychological construct, a subset of the hearer's assumptions' (Sperber and
Wilson 1986: 15). Originating in the mind of an asocial individual, this
amorphous body of information is neither socially nor discursively structured. In neither Sperber and Wilson nor in Grice is there any understanding of the way meanings, values, emotions, and truth-effects are shaped
and constrained by genre, and both their general principles (cooperation,
relevance) and the more specific maxims are too sweeping to explain how
particular kinds of information are implied in particular contexts.

The use of genre is one of the processes by which the background
knowledges brought into play by texts are given contextual shape and
focus. Genre is a framework for processing information and for allowing
us to move between knowledge given directly in a text and other sets of
knowledge that are relevant to understanding it. In order now to begin
working out more clearly some of the consequences of bringing genre
into the picture, let me return to the news headline I discussed in
Chapter 1. The text reads as follows:

RAPE CASE
JUDGE IN
NEW STORM

In order to understand this text a reader will need to be able to draw
inferences on the basis of a range of information which is not explicitly

present in the text. As I use these terms, inferences drawn by readers are the interpretive actualisation of textual implications. To put this differently, the text *presupposes* certain kinds of knowledge. Here, cast in propositional form, are some of the inferences that I think are likely to be drawn from the background information structuring this text:

That:

1   *the story is important and urgent* [this is implied by some of the material features of the text such as the size and boldness of the type]
2   *the story is true* [this is implied by the grammatical mood of the utterance (a declarative mood carried by the suppressed verb)]
3   *the text describes events which are relevant because they take place in the reader's own social environment* [this is a generic assumption of relevance implied in the structure of the speech situation, where the reader is invoked as a member of a community of interests]
4   *readers and newspaper share a common framework of values which differentiates them from criminals* [a generic assumption of shared values is implied in the structure of the speech situation]
5   *'storm' means 'controversy' in this journalistic context* [the reader is assumed to possess a lexical knowledge which is activated when s/he disambiguates the metaphor]
6   *there was an old controversy that preceded the current one and is similar in kind to it* [this is a logical entailment of the antinomic structure of the adjective 'new': that is, the way it implicitly invokes its opposite]
7   *you the reader know about it because you live in a common world mediated to you by the media* [again, this is a logical entailment of the semantic structure of 'new' together with the implications of the shared speech situation]
8   *storms over judges exist, in the media, because of what is perceived to be their lenient sentencing practices* [this is a generically assumed cultural knowledge]
9   *these practices contradict the desire of the tabloid media and their audience for tougher sentencing of criminals* [again, a generically assumed cultural knowledge]

10 *the discrepancy between the values of the judge and those of the supposed community of newspaper and audience provokes moral indignation* [this is a logical implication of the semantic content of 'storm' together with the generic assumption of shared values which is implicit in the speech situation]

Taken together, these inferences allow an informed reader to rewrite the condensed text in a fuller, more fully meaningful form, something like this:

> *A Scottish or English judge who was previously involved in the trial of a rapist which was controversial because of the lenient sentence handed down to the perpetrator has become embroiled in further controversy. We, the newspaper and the community of decent people it represents, are indignant that this man [another assumption] is allowed to get away with acting in disregard of community expectations.*

I'm not suggesting, of course, that any conscious process of rewriting goes on in our heads in this rather cumbersome way. This rewritten sentence is merely a representation of the kind of sense we are likely to make of the headline in the instantaneous flash of understanding we experience as we read it. I should also stress again that there is no guarantee that we *will* understand it: as Sperber and Wilson put it, 'failures in communication are to be expected: what is mysterious and requires explanation is not failure but success' (Sperber and Wilson 1986: 45).

The interesting question here, I think, has to do with the *kinds* of implicit knowledge that are drawn on here, and with how they are structured in the act of reading. I identify the following levels at which implicit knowledges are invoked in the headline text:

- the semantic features of material, lexical and syntactic structures;
- the structure of the speech situation, and the assumption of the relevance of the information to the receiver;
- generically assumed cultural knowledges.

It is the third of these areas that is most clearly related to genre: 'knowledge' of a certain (moralistic) kind about judges is in some sense inscribed in the populist genres of the tabloid press, and sexualised crimes of violence are one of those genres' characteristic preoccupations. But the kinds of knowledge derived from the structure of the speech situation – that is, the assumption that the mere fact of address somehow binds together speaker and receiver in a relationship of solidarity and thus in a mutual structure of value – is likewise a part of the rhetorical strategy of the headline genre and the broader range of tabloid genres to which it belongs; and even at the lexical level, where we might assume that words are to some extent autonomous of their discursive organisation, it is clear that words like 'new', 'storm', and 'judge' take on a semantic coding which is specific to this genre and carries information that is not necessarily present in other discursive contexts. Similarly, the grammatical logic of the declarative mood takes on a force here ('this is true') that is deeply inflected by the genre in which it occurs. The specific information constructed by the text does not occur in isolation from the larger shaping performed by the generic framework.

GENRE AS SCHEMA

This generic framework constitutes the unsaid of texts, the organisation of information which lies latent in a shadowy region from which we draw it as we need it; it is information that we may not know we know, and that is not directly available for scrutiny. One way of understanding both the cognitive and the textual processes involved in the supplementation of given information by this broader frame of background knowledge is through the concept of the *schema*. In the language of psychology, a schema is a pattern underlying a surface phenomenon which allows us to understand that phenomenon. If I sketch a picture of a smiling face, turned sideways, by using a colon and a right bracket, as follows:

:)

you know how to read this schematic text because you have studied faces since infancy, you can infer the structure of the face as a whole from this brief indication of 'eyes' and 'mouth', and you know as well the typographical conventions that have turned this sketch into an 'emoticon', the 'smile' command in a text-message. Every sighted human being has a store of experience of faces which has been converted into knowledge about faces in general, a set of expectations about their form which allows the conversion of these slight, schematic indications into the general form of the human face. The schema is what allows us to infer the whole from the part, the kind of thing this is from the representation of a few of its scattered features.

To speak of the schema is to assume that *knowledge is organised*, and thus that 'when we know something about a given domain, our knowledge does not consist of a list of unconnected facts, but coheres in specifiable ways' (Mandler 1984: ix). Genre is one of the forms that that organisation takes, making patterns of meaning relative to particular communicative functions and situations. This is partly no more than a matter of economy: if I'm reading a newspaper headline in the street, I don't need to have in my mind the information that would be relevant to reading a gothic romance or the instructions on a bureaucratic document, although I can activate that information should it become relevant. Genre cues act rather like context-sensitive drop-down menus in a computer program, directing me to the layers and sub-layers of information that respond to my purposes as a speaker or a reader or a viewer.

One could think of this information as being something like a combined encyclopaedia and dictionary, broken down into sub-sections for particular genres, in such a way that the genres of the tabloid press will have entries for 'judge' ('lenient on crime') 'new', 'storm', and 'rape' (situated somewhere close to 'paedophilia', but with a sub-entry referring the reader to 'rape – false accusations of'). The French theorist Jean-Jacques Lecercle says of this encyclopaedic organisation of cultural knowledge that it relates meanings to sets of contexts by guiding and constraining the reader's inferences from the text. But this is not to say that this information, these generically organised knowledges, exist in some mental cupboard as ready-formed resources, since they are 'not only a *body* of knowledge and belief, but also the operation that, in a context, selects the relevant information and gives it computable shape, or from a text infers a relevant context' (Lecercle 1999: 203). Rather than taking the form of explicit and articulated propositions, they are something like an emergent form, the result of use rather than pre-existing it. The cognitive scientist

Walter Kintsch represents this by speaking of knowledge as being made up of associative networks, 'knowledge nets', the nodes of which are 'propositions, schemas, frames, scripts, production rules'. Such nets are at once stable and yet, in practice, flexible and adaptable:

> Psychologically, only those nodes that are actually active (that is, are held in working memory) contribute to the meaning of a node. Because the capacity of working memory is severely limited, any node at any point in time has only a few neighbours; its meaning is sparse, therefore. However, it can be readily elaborated, almost without limit, in many different directions, as the situation demands, because most nodes in a knowledge network are connected with powerful, stable links – retrieval structures – to other nodes in the net that can be brought into working memory. Thus, very complex meanings can be generated automatically and effortlessly, although at any particular time only a few nodes can be active in working memory.
>
> (Kintsch 1998: 74)

Knowledge nets allow, then, for the activation on an *ad hoc* basis of relevant knowledges, distributing resources at any point in time between a foreground of active meanings and a more stable, although still constantly changing, background of encyclopaedic knowledge and beliefs. I take these knowledge nets to be in part generically organised, although Kintsch speaks only briefly of the organisational role of genre. Concepts, on this model, do not have a fixed and permanent meaning: rather, 'the context of use determines which nodes linked to a concept are activated when a concept is used' (Kintsch 1998: 75). For example, which properties of words like 'piano' or 'tomato' are activated depends on the discursive context, which may be that of music or of furniture-moving, of painting or of eating: and again I want to add that these are, in the broadest sense, generic contexts.

'Comprehension', Kintsch writes, 'implies forming coherent wholes with Gestalt-like qualities out of elementary perceptual and conceptual features' (Kintsch 1998: 93). Coherent wholes of this sort can be formed at different levels, but at the level of the generic frame they correspond to what I have called projected worlds. By 'world' I mean a relatively bounded and schematic domain of meanings, values, and affects, accompanied by a set of instructions for handling them. Seitel similarly speaks of 'generic worlds' as having the dimensions of 'time, space, categories of actors and settings, causality, and motivation – and the interpretation they call for' (Seitel 2003: 279). Any world can be described through a coherent set of propositions, and generates reality-effects specific to it: some worlds claim a high reality status, others announce themselves as fictional or hypothetical. Examples of such generically projected worlds would be:

- the world of the tabloid press, populated by celebrities, criminals, victims, nude models, and scenarios centred on scandal, crime, and sport. Its moral tone tends to be at once moralistic and salacious, and its time is that of a static continuum punctured by arbitrary events;

- the world of the picaresque novel, a world of sharp-witted servants and dull masters, of confidence tricks, of hunger and the constant threat of poverty, of the road and the unforeseen adventure, of upward and downward mobility, of a time which is at once episodic and recurrent;

- the world of the Petrarchan sonnet, where lovers are constant and fair mistresses are not, where suffering or bliss are the poles between which love moves, where eyes shoot beams to twine souls together, and where time is that of biological decay and its transcendence in love or in writing;

- the world of the curse: an emotionally narrow world defined – although it may not be lacking in wit or humour – by its simple, antagonistic structure of address and by the copiousness of imagined destinies or projected comparisons (usually from inferior realms) with which it expresses it; its time is the pure present of address, although it envisages a future that leads from it;

- the world of the television sitcom, perhaps best organised into its regional variants (New York, London's East End, small-town Australia, the cities of Brazil): a world structured around generational and sexual relationships, set in the household or some expanded form of the household (the pub, a hotel) and developing the narrative temporality of the 'relationship problem' (or, in a more sophisticated version, the 'social issue').

And so on, as many worlds as genres. The concept of 'world' as I use it here has affinities with Alfred Schutz's concept of 'finite provinces of meaning' (Schutz 1970: 252), although Schutz defines these provinces as experiential rather than representational. Every genre is defined in part by the bounded province of meaning which is specific to it and which it makes available for use.

GENERIC TRUTHS: PHILOSOPHY

In the rest of this chapter I look in more depth at the way different genres 'systematically form the objects of which they speak' (Foucault 1989: 49). My concern is with the effects of reality, of authority, of plausibility – in short, of truth – that are generated by the diverse genres of human communication. I shall talk briefly about two of the 'realist' genres that have been so important in the making of our world: those of philosophy and history. Robyn Ferrell writes that it is here that the full force of generic shaping is felt –

> in those genres whose trait is a constitutional *naïveté*, the trait of the transparency of their own means of representation. In this category can be found genres aimed at truthtelling (like some philosophy); the revealing of reality 'as it is' (empirical sciences of physical or social types); and, in general, genres of writing aimed at representing something without reference to the possibility of its representation. ... The means of representation in this large class of genres cannot become visible in the text without compromising its realist effect.
>
> (Ferrell 2002: 4)

But all genres, even those that Ferrell describes as being concerned with verisimilitude rather than veracity, and of course including the genre of theoretical argument in relation to which this book is written, work with such effects of authority and truth, embedded in their structure as much as they are worked out in the rhetoric of texts.

I begin with a book written in (or better, *writing*) one of the many genres of philosophy and which explores, in its own way, the concept of 'world' that I have taken from rather different discourses. This is David Lewis's *On the Plurality of Worlds*, an influential work of analytic philosophy published in 1986 as a defence of the concept of 'modal realism: the thesis that the world we are part of is but one of a plurality of worlds, and that we who inhabit this world are only a few out of all the inhabitants of all the worlds' (Lewis 1986: vii). In this fragment of a sentence we can see clearly the two languages from which the book is composed: a technical philosophical term is restated in plain language, although much of this plainness is deliberately and ironically deceptive: 'world' and 'is' by no means carry their everyday meaning here. Another way of thinking about this intersection of languages would be in terms of the distinction Freadman draws between the genres of metaphysics and logic. This distinction is not yet properly in play here, because both of the languages deployed in this sentence belong to 'metaphysics', 'the genre that denies its own generic specificity' (Freadman 2004: 6); but as the book develops it becomes clear that there is a tension between two different ways in which 'worlds' can be said to exist: a logical sense in which anything that can be posited can be said to have being, and another sense which is both that of metaphysics and that of 'plain' understanding, which is less willing to concede the existence of hypothetical or formally possible worlds.

A thesis, such as the one on modal realism that Lewis defends, is an argument which may turn out to be true. This is what philosophy does: it seeks truth, without being sure in advance that it will reach it. Lewis proposes nothing more than a statement of reasons for his position and of why they might be compelling, 'but I do not think that these reasons are conclusive' (Lewis 1986: viii). His strongest argument is a pragmatic one: there are many ways in which 'systematic philosophy goes more easily if we may presuppose modal realism in our analyses. I take this to be a good reason to think that modal realism is true, just as the utility of set theory in mathematics is a good reason to think that there are sets' (Lewis 1986: vii). The rhetorical force of his position is generated in part by a showing of modesty and by a use of the pronoun 'I' which points to the testing of argument against personal experience and an awareness of the fallibility of reason. At the same time the appeal to mathematics lays claim to the authority of a language which has always embodied for philosophy a superior rationality: Lewis's sets are, for all the differences, of the same order of being as the Platonic forms: timeless essences underlying and informing ever more mundane level of being.

Other worlds exist; 'there are' such worlds, each of them fully fur-
nished with things. But they do not exist in time and space: they are
neither near nor far, exist neither now nor at some other time. Their
mode of existence is thus not that of ordinary being, which happens in
space and time, but rather that of beings which are possible or conceivable: 'absolutely *every* way that a world could possibly be is a way
that some world *is*' (Lewis 1986: 2). The force of that 'is' now becomes
apparent. Lewis's thesis is a way of saying: for every possible state of
things let us suppose a world that corresponds to it. This thesis is
ironical, and the irony plays around the 'is' that designates virtuality
rather than factuality. It's a matter of definition: existence is here
taken to include the virtual, a position which contradicts commonsense assumptions but which makes sense in terms of another language, that of formal logic. This broadened definition is a tool that
does substantial work. Beginning with 'the familiar analysis of necessity as truth at all possible worlds' (Lewis 1986: 3), philosophy has
moved on to explore the heuristic force of counterfactuals, entities
which are not but could be. 'As the realm of sets is for the mathemati-
cian, so logical space is a paradise for philosophers': acceptance of the
'literal truth' of *possibilia*, things that are possible, is the price that
must be paid for gaining 'the wherewithal to reduce the diversity of
notions we must accept as primitive, and thereby to improve the unity
and economy of the theory that is our professional concern' (Lewis
1986: 4).

'Our professional concern' is what is at stake here, and what concerns
the community of philosophers is not just a set of questions about the
nature of things. If genres are, as I have argued, a matter of typified
rhetorical action, then the genres of philosophy are not only organisations of representation ('is this statement true about the world?') but
also practices of authorisation. They produce an authority in the very act
of discussing truth, and this practice happens both in each individual
act of philosophising and as a more general consolidation of the institutional authority of philosophy. It is to this consolidation that philosophers refer when they speak of their activity as a 'way of life' or a *paideia*,
a making-perfect through cumulative learning.

Lewis's argument, then, is that other worlds 'exist' in 'logical space',
and they are useful tools for exploring it. Here – to conclude my analysis

at the very beginning of Lewis's book – is an example of how the concept works for a discussion of modality:

> Other worlds are other, that is *un*actualised, possibilities. If there are many worlds, and every way that a world could possibly be is a way that some world is, then whenever such-and-such might be the case, there is some world where such-and-such is the case. Conversely, since it is safe to say that no world is any way that a world could not possibly be, whenever there is some world at which such-and-such is the case, then it might be [i.e., in the 'actual' world] that such-and-such is the case. So modality turns into quantification: possibly there are blue swans if [if and only if], for some world W, at W there are blue swans.
>
> (Lewis 1986: 5)

The language of formal logic employed here, with its productive reliance on tautology, is characteristic of the forms of argument deployed throughout the rest of the book: argument which seeks to respond to possible objections, to differentiate this version of the thesis from others, and to follow through some of its implications. The language is that of a relentlessly close reasoning which pursues a syllogism from its premises to its conclusions, sundering the true from the false or absurd.

Ferrell distinguishes three main genres structuring the language of philosophy: the dialogue, the confession, and the technical paper. Elements of each are present in *On the Plurality of Worlds*: the dialogue in the Preface's acknowledgement of friends and colleagues and in the close engagement with criticisms and objections; the confession in the deployment of the *topos* of modesty and of the first-person pronoun; and the technical paper in the use of formal logic. As I indicated before, there is a tension between the 'plain' language of the confession and the technical language of formal logic, and thus between the different conceptions of existence which correspond to each: the two forms of talk are initially fused and then become separate and even antagonistic. It is irony which at once masks and justifies the conflation of 'plain' and 'technical' languages, an irony which, like the *topos* of modesty, is inscribed in philosophy from Socrates onward and which, in conjunction with the display of close ratiocination, grounds the authority with which this book, and with which much of contemporary analytic philosophy, is able to speak.

There are, however, other ways of speaking about other worlds. One of them, at once closely parallel to this and quite radically distinct from it, is the group of poems in the first section of Jacques Roubaud's *The Plurality of Worlds of Lewis*, published in French in 1991. Roubaud, too, speaks by means of a certain mode of irony: the thesis of the plurality of worlds is a device, an enabling fiction, by which to meditate upon non-being, specifically the non-being of his dead wife. Roubaud takes from Lewis the promise that nothing that is conceivable is non-existent, and supposes that death is a virtual state which is other than the state of being which is life but which nevertheless 'exists'. Death is a counterfactual, and the dead inhabit that 'world' which logically corresponds to their special **ontology**. In a sense this is a consolation, but also not, because 'there is no transworld travel' (Roubaud 1995: 13); worlds do not overlap:

> One cannot cross from one sub-world to another,   one cannot cross alive.   or dead.

In return, however:

> you are,   are   there,   still.   It is the only consolation. Survival is too big a word.

> (Roubaud 1995: 35)

But how difficult it is to pronounce that contradictory 'you are': the 'you' that the poet speaks is the impossibility of which we know that:

> nothing impossible can be said
> otherwise, elsewhere
> except by saying.

> (Roubaud 1995: 30)

And the 'are' is that existence which continues, not by analogy with the body that the dead woman once was, and not in the memory of others, but rather in a repeated loss of being in memory: 'each time I think of you, you cease to be' (Roubaud 1995: 40). Non-being is that form of being that is not. But since it nevertheless *is*, then the being of our own world is called into question:

> for so many reasons this world, ours
> is impossible
>
> how can it be an instance of what should
>   be so that a world could be?
>
> but if there are many worlds, and every
>   way that a world could possibly be is a way
>   that some world   is
>
> if whenever such-and-such might
>   be the case
>
> there is some world then where
>   such-and-such is,
>
> this world, ours, the least likely, is possible:
>
> but reading it on this void does not mean I believe it.
> (Roubaud 1995: 23)

The poem takes the philosopher's words, intonations, and syntax and fills them with a quite different force. Its reality-effects, grounded in the peculiar suspension or distancing of reference that, within the appropriate generic frame, we attribute to poetic speech, turns the concept of world into something else again: neither actuality nor logical space but a metaphor for the speaking of death and for the experiential meanings of that speaking. Like the philosophical text, the poem speaks its truths through a logic that is embedded deep in its generic norms.

GENERIC TRUTHS: HISTORY

Rosalie Colie thinks of genres as 'a "set" on the world, as definitions of manageable boundaries, some large, some small, in which material can be treated and considered'; part of their force resides in the fact that, 'these sets and boundaries understood, a great deal need *not* be said about them' (Colie 1973: 115). To speak of genre is to speak of what need not be said because it is already so forcefully presupposed. Thus, she continues, 'the kinds can easily be seen as tiny subcultures with their own habits, habitats, and structures of ideas as well as their own forms' (Colie 1973: 116). The 'set', the cluster of attitudes and perspectives and ways of making sense of things, is a function of the boundaries that genre defines and to which we become habituated. Genres frame the world as a certain kind of thing, and we notice this framing only at its intersection with other subcultures of meaning.

I shall conclude this chapter by speaking briefly of the genres of history: a broad plurality of genres, certainly, that Phillips identifies as 'a cluster of overlapping and competing genres, "low" as well as "high" ' (Phillips 2003: 213), yet with a common set on the world that shapes what counts as properly historical knowledge.

Aristotle contrasts history with poetry by saying that 'the poet's function is to describe, not the thing that has happened, but a kind of thing that might happen'; the statements of poetry 'are of the nature rather of universals, whereas those of history are singulars' (Aristotle 1941: 1451). Yet in another sense the writing of history has always been characterised by a tension between the singularity of facts and their organisation into the patterns of narrative explanation, with all the questions of causality and necessity that arise from this patterning.

The singular fact is defined on the one hand by its ontological status: its factuality is a matter of evidence, established by procedures of authentication. On the other hand it is defined by its temporal status: it is complete and self-contained, and it is distinct both from the flow of insignificant events and from the present from which it is observed. Michel de Certeau would argue that the constitution of the singular fact as true and as past is the result of a single, **performative** operation: historiography's fundamental act is to take certain traces of the past, such as stories, bills of lading, letters, government edicts, scratchings on stone, and to separate them from the present in which they have survived. In general, he writes,

> every story that relates what is happening or what has happened constitutes something real to the extent that it pretends to be the

> representative of a past reality. It takes on authority by passing itself
> off as the witness of what is or of what has been. It seduces, and it
> imposes itself, under a title of events; which it pretends to interpret. ...
> In effect, every authority bases itself on the notion of the 'real', which
> it is supposed to recount.
>
> (Certeau 1986: 203)

Thus interpretation appears to follow from facts, which in fact it
constitutes as such; and time is conceived as a property of the object, the
past, but not of the present from which the historian speaks. Hence
the characteristic formal structure of historical narrative: the relating of
a closed and self-contained event or series of events in the preterite tense
('he went'), the third person, and from the impossible perspective of an
omniscient and unsituated narrator.

But to speak of a 'characteristic formal structure' is to simplify the
range of ways in which history is and has been written. A better starting
point might be to consider some of the 'simple forms' in which the past
has been constructed. A crucial distinction here is between sacred and
secular forms of writing: the setting of past events in relation to some
other, transcendental time, or in relation only to other mundane times.
In the proto-historical genre of genealogy, for example, the reconstruction of a chain of descent has the effect of setting the present in relation
not only to the line of forebears but also in relation to an order of kinship which is partly political and partly cosmological. The genealogy of
Christ recorded in *Matthew I* concludes with the following verse: '17: So
all the generations from Abraham to David are fourteen generations;
and from David until the carrying away into Babylon are fourteen generations; and from the carrying away into Babylon unto Christ are fourteen generations'. The point here, despite Joseph's genetic irrelevance, is
the placing of Christ in a direct line of descent from David and the
reconstruction of a mythical origin which repeats itself: the historical
event, the birth of Christ, is a repetition or a return which is acted out
in accordance with scriptural prophecy. Although there is one point at
which this genealogy intersects with historical time, that of the carrying
away into Babylon, the point again is not so much the fact of that historical event as its prefiguring of a repetition in which Christ will fulfil
the scriptures by leading his people out of bondage. The time of the

genealogy is a ritualisation of the time of memory, and the evocation of an underlying divine pattern in the succession of generations.

Other 'simple forms' of historical narrative include the eyewitness testimony, the reminiscence, the annal, and its more complex form, the chronicle. The first two of these stress the authentication of evidence over questions of pattern. They differ in that, whereas the eyewitness account tells a story to someone in a position of interest or authority – a judge, someone who has personal reasons for wanting to know the truth, or the historian collecting evidence – the reminiscence by contrast satisfies a need of the story's teller, often a need to reconcile past and present. As first-person narratives they possess the authenticity of direct vision, which is why the eyewitness is so important in issues of legal proof; but they thereby lack the comprehensive view of the detached observer, which is why they are usually no more than the raw materials of history.

The annal is perhaps the simplest form of such detached recording. Here, temporal order is given in the rigid and arbitrary form of chronology: the names of the consuls or the year of the king's reign are the container for a series of events which may have no other necessary relationship than this shared period of occurrence. Yet with even the simplest annal the stories begin to swell beyond this border to encompass other narrative forms. This is the story of Thomas à Becket from Capgrave's mid-fifteenth-century *Chronicle of England* (Capgrave 1858: 140):

> In the VII. yere of Herry deied Theobald bischop of Cauntirbury; and Thomas, the Kyngis Chauncelere, entred into that benefice. Aftir that fel gret strif betwix him and the Kyng for liberty of the Cherch; for whech first was the bischop exiled, and many wrongis do to him and to his kyn. Thanne cam he hom ageyn, and was killid, as alle the nacion knowith; and this was in the yere of oure Lord a M.CLXX.

The narrative of Becket's tenure of the bishopric covers a period of nine years, but this period is presented as though it belonged to a single entry in either one of the organising chronologies: the years of the king's reign, or anno domini. The narrative is an incoherent mix of seriality ('aftir ... thanne') and causality ('for whech'), together with moral commentary ('many wrongis') and appeal to consensual knowledge. Here by contrast is a narrative of great temporal and causal complexity, the second paragraph of Tacitus's *Annals*:

> When after the destruction of Brutus and Cassius there was no longer any army of the commonwealth, when Pompeius was crushed in Sicily, and when, with Lepidus pushed aside and Antonius slain, even the Julian faction had only Caesar left to lead it, then, dropping the title of triumvir, and giving out that he was a consul, and was satisfied with a tribune's authority for the protection of the people, Augustus won over the soldiers with gifts, the populace with cheap corn, and all men with the sweets of repose, and so grew greater by degrees, while he concentrated in himself the functions of the Senate, the magistrates, and the laws. He was wholly unopposed, for the boldest spirits had fallen in battle, or in the proscription, while the remaining nobles, the readier they were to be slaves, were raised the higher by wealth and promotion, so that, aggrandised by revolution, they preferred the safety of the present to the dangerous past.

(Tacitus 1964: 3–4)

The structure of the syntax in the first sentence ('When … when … and when … then'; Tacitus's Latin, after an initial 'postquam', 'after', uses a set of terse ablative absolutes) pulls together three times: that of the battles and deaths of the civil wars; a subsequent state of affairs in which 'there was no longer any army' and the Julian faction had no other leader; and the time of Augustus's actions as a result of this state. These interwoven times move from past to present; the second sentence reverses this temporal direction, moving from the present to the past then back again. In addition, there is a third, unstated order of time at work here, that of the narration. In each of the times described a series of facts is drawn together to form an account of a state of affairs, and these states are then linked in causal chains. The first chain leads from the defeat of Augustus's opponents in the civil wars to the resulting power vacuum, the bribery of the soldiers and populace, and finally Augustus's usurpation of power. The second chain repeats the first with variations, adding to the account of the power vacuum the further explanation of the compliance of the nobility as a result of their weakening and their openness to bribery. The actors here are either individuals representing larger forces (not just

Brutus and Cassius were defeated, but by extension the armies that gave them their power), or they are classes (the nobility, the soldiers, and the populace are not individualised because they have no leaders who can stand for the class). All of this answers the question: what were the circumstances that allowed Augustus to accede to power? The answer, given in terms of a series of *events* which produce *states of affairs* which make possible further *events*, thus interweaves narrative with analysis. This, we might say, is the classic task of the genres of history: to trace the movements and the causal interactions between event and structure, transforming document into narrative and narrative into explanation.

The critical order of time for the production of these effects is the unstated present of narration from which past orders are projected as domains of facticity. Tacitus does of course situate himself in this present, but only negatively: it is his distance from the past that allows him to write *sine ira et studio*, without bitterness or partisanship. Temporal distance, the severing of the past from the present, is what makes possible the passage from documentary evidence to established historical fact.

From Tacitus to the historians of the modern world is a large step. Two hundred years of historicism, permeating all dimensions of thought, and a similarly long period of methodological reflection and refinement, have transformed the foundations of history as a discipline. Some of the extraordinary diversity of forms of writing over these two centuries has been explored by writers like Hayden White, although his approach is very different from mine. Yet much too has remained constant in that 'telling of history' which 'is filtered through the genres in which it occurs' (Hanks 1996: 269).

My final text is a passage from Fernand Braudel's great history of *The Mediterranean and the Mediterranean World in the Age of Philip II*, published in 1949 and in a revised second edition in 1966:

> Further light will no doubt be shed on the question by future historians using evidence of a rather different order. In Venice, which I have personally studied in some detail, I am impressed, for example, by the scale of public building and decoration in the city after 1450: the replacement of the wooden bridges over the canals by stone bridges, the digging of the great well near the church of Santa Maria di Brolio

in August, 1445, the construction in May, 1459 of a new loggia *in loco Rivoalto*, where the weavers' shops were demolished to make way for the extension to the Doges' Palace. ... Needless to say, this evidence does not prove anything one way or the other, either in Venice (where construction may have been carried out because or in spite of the economic climate) or in the Mediterranean as a whole. But it inclines me to classify the whole vigorous period from 1450 to 1650 as a unit, the 'long' sixteenth century, and therefore to agree with Jean Fourastié and his pupils that the first wave of prosperity was independent of American bullion. To take a single city, in this case Venice, as an index, can be a fruitful exercise; it may even reveal a truer picture of the economic situation than we have from price curves.

(Braudel 1973: II, 894–5)

A couple of brief observations on this small excerpt from a massive work. The first has to do with Braudel's remarks on questions of evidence, where, far from concealing himself from view, the writer constantly intervenes in his own person to comment on the validity of the data available to him and on the need to refine the tools used by the historian. The machinery of source critique and of the interpretive construction of evidence from documents is here fully in view: there is no attempt, as de Certeau would have it, to conceal the institutional apparatus within which Braudel works.

The second comment has to do with the role of singularity in this text: the mention of the 'great well near the church of Santa Maria di Brolio', this tiny and locally specific detail in a sweeping argument, is part of a process by which the author develops a claim to rhetorical authority by building a 'world' out of such particulars grafted on to the larger architecture of structural analysis. It's a kind of claim to omniscience, grounded in the amassing of evidence from primary sources and the sheer labour that it involves; and it is a claim to truth in so far as these details, like the realist novel's *petit fait vrai* (the small, convincing detail), stand for something like the irreducibility of the real.

The third comment concerns dating. The building of the stone bridges, the well, and the loggia are tiny events fitted into the broader chronology of the 'long sixteenth century' which can be understood as a slowly developing structure. It is the play of event and structure, the moment and the long duration, narrative and explanation that provides the backbone of the book, with its interplay of the times of environmental history (or geography), of social history, and of rapidly occurring historical events (Braudel 1972: I, 20–1). At the heart of this dialectic is the historical *period* – whether understood as the reign of Philip II or as the 'long' sixteenth century – where 'the different measures of time past' are brought together 'in all their multiplicity' in the writing of 'a new kind of history, *total history*' (Braudel 1973: II, 1238). It is this conception that is the object of Michel Foucault's criticism in *The Archaeology of Knowledge* when he writes of its supposition 'that one and the same form of historicity operates upon economic structures, social institutions and customs, the inertia of mental attitudes, technological practice, political behaviour', and that 'history itself may be articulated into great units – stages or phases – which contain within themselves their own principle of cohesion' (Foucault 1989: 9–10). Yet this does less than justice to Braudel's concern with the multiplicity of historical times and with the resistance of the event to explanation: there is rather a tension in his work between the heterogeneity of the event and the homogeneity of the historical period.

This tension is not dissimilar to that which we saw at work in Tacitus: the writing of history is generically structured by the narrative problems of binding the singularities of events and their multiplicity of times into the coherence of a structural explanation. Everything else follows from this: the grounding of the reality of the event in the authenticity of the primary source, the evaluative balancing of sources against each other, the striving for a 'unique, comprehensive view of the subject' (Braudel 1972: I, 354) in which individual perspectives will blend into the godlike vision of the writer who commands all knowledge: it is by such means that history seeks to move beyond – and thus confirms – the generically specific nature of its truths.

5

GENRE AND INTERPRETATION

READING GENRE

An email comes to me from the Federal Secretariat in Lagos, Nigeria, confiding in me that a Dr Akin Adesola and his colleagues wish to divert some funds to an account which he asks me to set up for them in my own country; in return for rendering this service I will be entitled to specify a certain percentage of these funds as my commission. His letter goes into some detail about the administrative arrangements that have made it possible for him and his colleagues to divert this money from its legitimate use, and he also tells me why it is not possible for him to set up the foreign account himself.

I read this email in one of two ways. It may be what it seems to be: a business letter addressed to a stranger soliciting his assistance. Or it may be the well-known Nigerian scam, the '419 Fraud' which has duped many thousands of naïve people out of their money. Since I have received a number of rather similar emails in the past, I suspect it may be the latter.

My interpretation involves the answers to two questions: first, 'what is it that's going on here?'; second, 'what kind of thing is this?' The second question is about the genre of this email, and when I have answered it I can then answer the first question: I know what's going on here.

Most decisions about texts aren't as straightforwardly either/or as this one, though; and in the case of more complex texts we may feel that 'reading for the genre' would be reductive of their detailed and subtle nuances. Genre analysis can look like a very blunt instrument to use on texts.

And indeed it would be, if all we cared about were identifying the genre to which a text 'belongs'. My argument, however, is that we read for something different: for an awareness of how the subtleties of texts are generically formed and governed. We read, consciously or unconsciously, for those layers of background knowledges which texts evoke and which are generically shaped and generically specific. This is where the real complexity of texts lies; if we are to read well, we cannot but attend to those embedded assumptions and understandings which are structured by the frameworks of genre and from which we work inferentially to the full range of textual meaning. Genre, as Beebee writes, 'is only secondarily an academic enterprise and a matter for literary scholarship. Primarily, genre is the precondition for the creation and the reading of texts' (Beebee 1994: 250).

Genre guides interpretation because it is a constraint on semiosis, the production of meaning; it specifies which types of meaning are relevant and appropriate in a particular context, and so makes certain senses of an utterance more probable, in the circumstances, than others. E.D. Hirsch has enunciated this interpretive role of genre with great clarity. In his understanding of it, genre is neither a collection of texts nor a set of lists of essential features of texts but an interpretive process called into being by the fact that 'all understanding of verbal meaning is necessarily genre-bound' (Hirsch 1967: 76). What he means by genre is the guess that we make about what kind of thing this is, and this guess, the interpreter's 'preliminary generic conception', is then 'constitutive of everything that he subsequently understands, and … this remains the case unless and until that generic conception is altered' (Hirsch 1967: 74). What we guess at is a determinate logic of implication, which then allows us to make appropriate inferences about meaning. Hirsch's case is flawed by his grounding of what he calls the 'intrinsic genre' of a text in the author's will or intention, which he understands as a norm yielding the possibility of a 'correct' interpretation. Yet since 'the intrinsic genre is always construed, that is, guessed, and is never in any important sense given' (Hirsch 1967: 88), this attempt to close off the multiplicity of interpretations seems like wishful thinking.

If we retain from Hirsch the notion that genre is a guess or construal of the-kind-of-thing-this-is, however, then it follows that genre is not a *property* of a text but is a function of reading. Genre is a category that we *impute* to texts, and under different circumstances this imputation may change. Think of the way different productions of a play, each involving the staging of an interpretation, may substantially alter the relevant genre framework. The telemovie of Trevor Nunn's 1976 staging of *Macbeth*, for example, with its terse, stripped-back text, sparse scenery, voice-overs, and close-ups, draws on television's capacity for intimacy and interiority to rewrite the text as a bleak psychological drama. Every such interpretation involves a shift in generic framework: the-kind-of-thing-this-is changes with its readings.

A radical statement of this dependence of genre schemata on our uses and interpretations of texts is given by Adena Rosmarin:

> Once genre is defined as pragmatic rather than natural, as defined rather than found, and as used rather than described, then there are precisely as many genres as we need, genres whose conceptual shape is precisely determined by that need. They are designed to serve the explanatory purpose of critical thought, not the other way around.
>
> (Rosmarin 1985: 25)

Thus 'genre is not, as is commonly thought, a class but, rather, a classifying statement' (Rosmarin 1985: 46). But where, we might ask, do these statements come from? From the minds of critics or readers? Surely the point is that genre norms are shared and shareable, and are built into more or less durable infrastructures. As Altman adds after citing the last sentence of Rosmarin's: 'we may fruitfully recognise the extent to which genres appear to be initiated, stabilised and protected by a series of institutions essential to the very existence of genres' (Altman 1999: 85).

Genre is neither a property of (and located 'in') texts, nor a projection of (and located 'in') readers; it exists as a part of the relationship between texts and readers, and it has a systemic existence. It is a shared convention with a social force. The imputations or guesses that we make about the appropriate and relevant conventions to apply in a particular case will structure our reading, guiding the course it will take, our expectations of what it will encounter. But they are grounded in the institutions in which genre has its social being: the institutions of classification in the broadest sense.

THE FRAME

A paddle steamer approaches a town on a broad river. There is music in the air, and as it gets closer I see and hear the playing of a steam organ on board the boat. Its tune merges with orchestral music, then as the boat nears the landing a troupe of performers break into song and dance. While they are in full song a band emerges from within the steamer, and I make the assumption that these players are the source of the music I have been hearing, and that the performance is advertising a show.

Some minutes later a gambler strolls from a tavern to the boat. I know that he is a professional gambler because he is playing cards in the morning, is dressed in morning suit and top hat, and has a thin moustache. Again, music fills the air and he breaks into song, wondering whether there is a place somewhere in the world for him. This music has no apparent source; it comes from nowhere, or at least from nowhere in the world shown on the screen.

If we had not already realised it, and if we have some familiarity with Hollywood movies, we are likely to hypothesise quite quickly that this is 'a particular kind of film in which otherwise unmotivated singing is likely to occur' (Neale 2000: 31–2). It is of course a musical – the 1951 version of *Showboat*. Like many musicals, it eases us into a world where people sing to full, invisible orchestral accompaniment, and it does so by initially tying this music to a visible source. Once it has made this move it then adopts the convention of spontaneous song and sourceless music. Our provisional hypothesis then 'offers grounds for further anticipation: if a film is a musical, more singing is likely, and the plot is liable to follow some directions rather than others' (Neale 2000: 32). But it also offers more basic information about what kind of world this is, and what counts as plausible in this world, although not in others. Here, unlike most other worlds, bursting into song is appropriate, probable, and thus believable; indeed, it is more or less obligatory within the genre.

Genre thus defines a set of expectations which guide our engagement with texts. It is oriented to the future. Drawing an analogy between speech genres and the anticipatory structure of sentences, Bakhtin expresses this orientation as follows:

> We learn to cast our speech in generic forms and, when hearing others' speech, we guess its genre from the very first words; we predict a certain length (that is, the approximate length of the speech whole) and a certain compositional structure; we foresee the end; that is, from the very beginning we have a sense of the speech whole, which is only later differentiated during the speech process.
>
> (Bakhtin 1986: 79)

This anticipatory structure is of course based on the cues we receive when we first encounter a text, and we could think of reading or viewing as a process of progressive refinement and adaptation of the sense we make of those cues. Heather Dubrow uses the analogy with the expectations set up by the prosodic pattern of a poem, establishing a contract with the reader that may be modified in the course of the textual encounter. The contract specifies both what may and what cannot happen in the text; but it is always the case that 'codes may be violated ... and contracts broken' (Dubrow 1982: 37). The cues that I encounter are **metacommunications**, then, specifying how to use the text, what one can expect to happen at different stages, and what to do if these expectations are not confirmed (for example, how to switch to a different generic framework).

Some cues are fully internal to the text. The laugh track on a television sitcom, although added in post-production, is integral to the working of the text, having the primary function of signalling genre and an absent but supposed genre community (Altman 1999: 160), and only secondarily of differentiating text segments. Many other cues are, however, located at the margins of texts.

It isn't often the case that I simply happen across a musical or a television sitcom, recognising it only from its internal cues. More usually, I encounter a range of cues located at the edge of the text. I read a review of the movie, I talk to other people about it, I read a poster advertising it in generic terms – although these terms may deliberately be left ambiguous in order to attract overlapping audiences – I know the cinema in which the movie is shown, and I read the title and the credits of actors and director. All of these things tend to effect a compelling pre-orientation to the film. Similarly, in the case of the television programme, even if I come across it without prior knowledge, without having read about it in a television guide, I know at least the time slot in which it is shown and the channel that screens it, with everything that this implies about the intended audience and thus about the kind of programme it is.

Genette has written extensively about the apparatus of external cues that surround a literary text: such things as the author's name, the book's title, the preface, and illustrations accompany the text 'precisely in order to *present* it, in the usual sense of this verb but also in the strongest sense: to *make present*, to ensure the text's presence in the world, its "reception" and consumption' (Genette 1997: 1). Many of these external cues, or *paratexts*, have to do with the material form of the book: even before we begin reading we are given information by the book's size and format, by its binding, by whether it has cut or uncut pages. If it is a pocket edition, or a 'classics' edition, or if it has a predominance of graphic material, then again we are disposed to read the book in certain ways. We make deductions from the author's name, if there is one, including any biographical material we may deduce from it, such as gender, or associate with it since we know it from elsewhere – perhaps from the dust jacket, or from reviews. Indications of the period in which the book was written are likely to be carried in this way. The title may give an indication of genre: *Henry IV, Part I* indicates a history play, even apart from the placing of this play with the 'Histories' in Shakespeare's first Folio; or it may carry a genre marker as a subordinate part: *Stamboul Train: An Entertainment* is Graham Greene's way of distinguishing between the thrillers and the 'serious' novels in his oeuvre, and thus of telling us how he wants them read. Blurbs, dedications and inscriptions, epigraphs, prefaces and postfaces, internal titles, tables of contents, running heads, notes, publicity materials – all of these seek to orient the reader towards an expectation of the kind of thing this is.

I have said that this apparatus is a set of cues that 'surround' or 'accompany' the text; but they are of course also a *part* of the text, and this ambiguity about their relation to it is crucial to the way such paratextual material works. Genette puts it this way:

> More than a boundary or a sealed border, the paratext is, rather, a *threshold*. ... It is an 'undefined zone' between the inside and the outside, a zone without any hard and fast boundary on either the inward side (turned toward the text) or the outward side (turned toward the world's discourse about the text), an edge, or, as Philippe Lejeune put it, 'a fringe of the printed text which in reality controls one's whole reading of the text'. Indeed, this fringe, always the conveyor of a commentary that is authorial or more or less legitimated by the author, constitutes a zone between text and off-text, a zone not only of transition but of *transaction*: a privileged place of a pragmatics and a strategy, of an influence on the public.
>
> (Genette 1997: 2)

The edge of the text is a site of dangerous ambivalence which must be negotiated and secured. In doing so the paratextual apparatus works as a *frame*, a word that I have used frequently in this book as a near-synonym of genre. Frames work to define the text against those things which it is not, cutting it off from the adjacent world; and to convey information from that adjacent world to the framed text. The frame belongs to both domains – both 'inside' and 'outside' – and to neither. Goffman thus distinguishes between two layers of frame:

> One is the innermost layering, wherein dramatic activity can be at play to engross the participant. The other is the outermost lamination, the *rim* of the frame, as it were, which tells us just what sort of status in the real world the activity has, whatever the complexity of the inner laminations.
>
> (Goffman 1974: 82)

And he later adds that 'the assumptions that cut an activity off from the external surround also mark the ways in which this activity is inevitably bound to the surrounding world' (Goffman 1974: 249).

The frame of course is unitary, neither inside nor outside, and this distinction of levels is a fiction to express the 'thickness' of the frame, its ambivalent duality as a component of structure and a component of situation. For a literary text it works both as an enclosure of the internal fictional space and as an exclusion of the space of reality against which the text is set; but this operation of exclusion is also an inclusion of the text within this alien space. The text is closed and suspended, but as a constructional element the frame is internal to this closure and through it the text signifies difference, signifies what it excludes. Within the field of vision are included both the aesthetic space and the edge of aesthetic space. The extra-aesthetic is manifested negatively at this moment of passage, where the text reaches the limit and starts to become non-text. The energy of the frame thus radiates in two directions simultaneously: on the one hand, it 'quotes' the text within a context where it is assigned a particular function; on the other, it conducts the trace of the excluded non-aesthetic area inward, so that the delimited space of the text is structured by its limit and becomes significant because of the restrictions operated by the frame. Thus the compositional structure of a painting – its perspective, the play of vectors, the foregrounding and backgrounding of motifs – is defined by the relation to the vertical and horizontal lines of the 'edge'; and these are not simply the farthest point to which the painting reaches but are rather the dynamic moments which constitute the system and the semantic richness of the painting.

To speak of the 'thickness' of the frame is a way of indicating the different degrees of generality at which a text is defined: its placing, for example, as an act of communication, as an aesthetic or non-aesthetic text, and as a text working in or on a particular genre and sub-genre. We could thus think of the 'edge' of the work as being something like a series of concentric waves in which the textual space is enclosed. Cinematic space is marked by the screen, by the darkness that surrounds the screen, by the projection apparatus and the theatre situation, and by advertisements, billings and reviews that constitute the visible frame of the industry. There is also an internal frame, the title sequence and credits, which supplements and narrows down the pre-definition of the kind of aesthetic space being outlined. (These two paragraphs are adapted from Frow 1986: 220–4.)

We could say, then, that the frame enclosing any piece of text is both a set of material determinants and a metaphor for the frame structure of genre. MacLachlan and Reid interrogate the force of the frame by asking how it is that we can identify certain texts as belonging to the genre of the epitaph, when there are no 'collective distinguishing marks' by which one can tell them from other kinds of text (MacLachlan and Reid 1994: 86). What does mark them off, of course, is that epitaphs are inscribed on gravestones. An inscription such as *'Tis I; be not afraid* signifies only by virtue of the place from which it is spoken, its 'framed occasion'. This utterance, for example, is likely to accompany the name and death-date of a deceased person, and to be found in a cemetery, where it marks a site of memory. This situation is at once physical and symbolic, marking 'a relevant semantic field of coherence – one that signifies mourning and consolation' (MacLachlan and Reid 1994: 87).

At the same time, the fact that these words are a quotation from words spoken by Jesus in an appearance to the disciples when he walked on water gives them an added layer of generic complexity: the 'I' who speaks belongs to the genre of the biblical parable as it is embedded in the genre of the epitaph, and this speaking position is thus projected outward from the 'I' of the dead person to that of Jesus, understood both as speaking to him or her in the afterlife and as speaking words of reassurance directly to the reader. The text is at once framed and, as citation, reframed in a double act of generic attribution.

Conversely, when the genre of the epitaph itself is cited, as happens when the literary epitaph pretends to refer to a tombstone on which it is inscribed, the genre changes: the 'simple form' of the epitaph, itself a variant of the lapidary inscription, becomes a more complex and layered form. This is Ben Jonson's *On my first Daughter*:

Here lyes to each her parents ruth,
Mary, the daughter of their youth:
Yet, all heavens gifts, being heavens due,
It makes the father, lesse, to rue.
At six moneths end, shee parted hence
With safetie of her innocence;
Whose soule heavens Queene, (whose name shee beares)
In comfort of her mothers teares,
Hath plac'd amongst her virgin-traine:
Where, while that sever'd doth remaine,
This grave partakes the fleshly birth.
Which cover lightly, gentle earth.

Although the generic indicator 'epitaph' is not given here, it is clear that the poem works in direct relation to it: 'here lyes' is the traditional *hic jacet* of the epitaph on a gravestone, a marker of place in the same way as is 'this grave' and the apostrophe to the earth above it. The contrast between the soul in heaven and the earthly remains is a central theme of the genre, and the beautiful syntactic intertwining in the first couplet of the parents' grief ('ruth') with the child's dead body similarly plays out the customary division between the dead and the living who mourn. Yet these words occur on the page of a book, and that makes all the difference to their status. Even had they occurred as well on Mary's gravestone, they are here, on the page, the imitation of an epitaph: 'the very same words that commemorate the dead person on that spot have another function if transcribed to a page. ... Their genre is literary: the effects they produce are those of a poem' (MacLachlan and Reid 1994: 89).

MacLachlan and Reid's argument is that 'genre, in a broad or narrow sense, is an effect of framing'. Yet we cannot conclude, as Rosmarin's nominalist argument would seem to suggest, that interpreters have licence to read whatever generic form they please into a text. Rather, the way we assign a text to a genre 'will depend not only on the framing impulses of interpreters but also on promptings by the text and the text's situation' – promptings or cues which 'may take the form of a distinctive typographic pattern of words on a page, a line drawn around an exhibit in a gallery, the relocation of an object in a new space that gives it a different semiotic charge, and so on' (MacLachlan and Reid 1994: 91). These cues are in one sense, as Genette indicates, a matter of authorial intention (Genette 1997: 408), although this is not to say that these guidelines must be respected. In a more profound sense, however, neither authors nor readers act as autonomous agents in relation to the structures of genre, since these structures are the shared property of a community. Readers and writers negotiate the generic status of particular texts but do not have the power to make their ascriptions an inherent property of those texts.

GENERIC CUES

Let me now turn to begin exploring the 'internal' cues that provide a set of continuing instructions on how to use a text. I want to look in

particular at ways in which these instructions may be modified or transformed as the text shifts or complicates its generic orientation.

My first text is a traditional nursery rhyme:

> There was a man of double deed
> Sowed his garden full of seed.
> When the seed began to grow,
> 'Twas like a garden full of snow;
> When the snow began to melt,
> 'Twas like a ship without a belt;
> When the ship began to sail,
> 'Twas like a bird without a tail;
> When the bird began to fly,
> 'Twas like an eagle in the sky;
> When the sky began to roar,
> 'Twas like a lion at the door;
> When the door began to crack,
> 'Twas like a stick across my back;
> When my back began to smart,
> 'Twas like a penknife in my heart;
> When my heart began to bleed,
> 'Twas death and death and death indeed.

The genre of the nursery rhyme is defined above all by its situation
of address: it is characteristically spoken or sung, to or by a child, and is
usually short, strongly rhythmical, and may involve a play with non-
sense words; it may accompany such activities as skipping, clapping or
counting, or being sung to sleep. In a sense it is a conglomerate genre,
and may include such kinds as ballads, riddles, proverbs, street cries,
skipping songs, lullabies, or counting-out rhymes. Because it often proceeds by word-association or by a play on sound, its logic is often close
to that of dreams.

The formal structure of this text is that of a series of rhyming couplets, the last one repeating the rhyme of the first, with alternating
iambic and trochaic lines; the initial pattern of iambic/trochaic is
reversed for the other couplets. A succession of **figures** (similes) is liter-
alised in each succeeding couplet; or, more precisely, one of the nouns

mentioned in the figure takes on a reality in the next couplet, in turn generating further figures until the final couplet in which the emphatically repeated noun 'death' works as the end of **figuration**. The poem thus moves from figural transformation to the non-figurative real, and from verbal play to pain and death.

It is possible to read a form of narrative coherence into the poem by reading it as a moral fable deducing the consequences that flow from the action of the man of double deed. This reading is supported by the fact that the first couplet is similar to an existing moral proverb ('A man of words and not of deeds/ Is like a garden full of weeds'), cited by Iona and Peter Opie in their edition of the *Oxford Dictionary of Nursery Rhymes* (Opie 1952: 286). Yet this narrative coherence has little to do with the logic that drives the poem and gives it its real force: a logic of the unstoppable causal chain in which words are imagined and then become real, inexorably taking on a life of their own which culminates in the sudden turn from third- to first-person and the death of the speaker. In generic terms we could say either that the genre of the moral proverb is transformed into a dream-narrative, or that the child's nursery rhyme becomes a statement of metaphysical despair in which the speaker imagines and experiences his own death. The cues given to the reader here are those of the poem's dream logic of ontological transformation (strongly resembling the nightmarish transformations of Kafka's 'A Country Doctor') and, in particular, its ultimate reversal in the bleak finality of the last line. The Opies mention that the poem is known in some versions as a riddle, and also that it is 'very similar to a ball-bouncing song sent by a correspondent in 1946' (Opie 1952: 287) – which might explain something of its inexorability. But we could also say – as I'm inclined to – that in fusing quite incompatible genres this poem successfully defies generic classification. The point, in any case, is not to assign it to one or more genres, but rather to notice its provocation of the question about what kind of thing this is, a provocation which, however forcefully it unsettles generic norms, never takes us to some point beyond that question.

My next example returns me to a closer reading of the opening sequence of *Showboat*. Here we are surely in no doubt that the movie is defined by the genre of the musical. But what it means for a movie to be 'in' or to 'belong to' a genre is a more complicated matter.

The credit sequence begins with text screened over a series of shots of the Mississippi taken at different times of day and night. During this sequence the screen is bordered by a curlicued gilt picture frame, as is our initial view of the paddle steamer, which we see in a still shot framed behind an old paddle wheel in the lower right corner. The boat then begins to move and the gilt frame fades away as the movie proper begins.

The following sequence works as a kind of non-narrative prologue. A rapid collage of establishing shots shows us fields and a town on the banks of the river. Black men and women are picking cotton in the fields, a black man is fishing from a boat, the white gentry are picnicking in the grounds of the plantation houses. A boy rides a mule through the fields, passing a man piling cotton into a wagon, to tell everyone he passes 'here comes the showboat!'. As the music, a medley of songs from the film, gathers in intensity, streams of people flow towards the town to welcome the boat, and we then move into the following sequence.

This opening movement works with a kind of choreographed energy as it pulls together the diversity of scenes and social levels into a single pulsing stream. It contrasts with a quite different form of representation punctuating it: a series of well-composed framing shots, picking up the initial view of the steamer, in which the boat is seen, in saturated Technicolor, framed by trees and reflected in the water, or framed by the pillars of a veranda. The structure of these shots is repeated at the close of the movie, when in a double movement the boat is framed first by the kiss of the reunited lovers, and then by the figure of the outcast Julie giving them her blessing.

The opening sequence, establishing the relationship between the boat and the land, is followed by a song-and-dance number that flows from the steamer onto the dock; it culminates in Captain Andy's trumpet fanfare, and his introduction of the performers. This is close to the 'putting on a show' sub-genre of the musical, and it has some of the core features of the Hollywood musical: the stylised coordination of bodies and voices, and a sexualised vitality which picks up on the choreographed energy of the flowing crowds and turns it into performance. We could say, then, that the opening sequences set up a contrast between two aesthetics: the show-business aesthetic of the song-and-dance routines, and the pictorial aesthetic of the well-composed framing shots.

A second major dichotomy has to do with the genre-associations of the shots of cotton fields, black labourers, and porticoed mansions. *Showboat* carries strong traces of two earlier films: the 1936 *Showboat* which it remakes, and *Gone with the Wind*, from 1939. The Southern setting, the costumes, even the physical appearance of Grayson and Keel, recall the period costume drama of *Gone with the Wind*, as does much of the plot. Where the musical is an inherently celebratory form, the drama here foregrounds the loss of love and the passage of time. In two counterposed plots, Magnolia Hawks and Gaylord Ravenal fall in love, lose each other, and are reunited some years later; while Julie LaVerne, the mulatto character played by Ava Gardner, is driven from the boat with her lover, is eventually deserted by him, and becomes an alcoholic.

The film thus counterposes two modes of temporality: the **kairos** of song, a time out of time, a moment of ecstatic intensity; and the **chronos** of time passing, of ageing and loss. These modes are in one sense internal to the musical, where they take the form of a tension between the *number*, standing outside of narrative time, and the passage of time in *narrative*; but they also correspond to the difference between the celebratory vitality of the musical and the time-bound world of the drama – between 'Saturday night' and 'Monday morning', as the Captain puts it.

Finally, music itself works in two rather different presentational modes in *Showboat*: on the one hand as public performance, integrated with dance and directly addressing an audience; on the other as a version of private thought. Gaylord Ravenal's first song, or his duet with Magnolia, 'Make Believe', are cast as the expression of a consciousness which we can overhear but which is invisible and inaudible to other characters; similarly, when the end of Warfield's rendition of 'Ol' Man River' coincides with the departure at dawn of Julie and her lover Steve, driven away by a charge of miscegenation, the camera identifies her with the weariness expressed by the song, as though it were coming from within her. The distinction between these two modes overlaps, although not completely, with another between 'music-hall' song and dance traditions, and what is called 'negro music', notably Julie's song, which Magnolia later makes her own, 'Can't Help Loving That Man of Mine'.

What I have been calling 'the musical', then, is not a unitary genre. Its core formal structure, the spectacle of the song-and-dance number, is modulated here by other functions, and its core aesthetic is challenged by other structures of value involving dramatic realism and introspection. Altman notes that the film moves between the three major sub-genres of the musical: the *fairy-tale musical*, in which 'the creation of an imaginary kingdom creates ample opportunity to stress the transcendence of the real that characterises the musical as a whole in comparison to other Hollywood genres'; the *show musical*, which 'maximises the genre's general expression of joy through music and dance'; and the *folk musical*, which 'plays up the togetherness and communitarianism characteristic of the genre' (Altman 1987: 126). These sub-genres correspond to three distinct modes of formation of the couple and the cultural plots they sustain: the restoration of order to the kingdom, the creation of a work of art, and the group's communion with itself and with the land; and to three kinds of fantasies of transcendence: being in another place (the fairy-tale kingdom), being in another body (the illusion of the stage), and being in another time (Altman 1987: 127). Split between these sub-genres, and between the genre as a whole and that of dramatic realism, *Showboat* is at once marked by generic heterogeneity and yet central to the tradition of the Hollywood musical. The intertextual cues guiding our understanding of the logic of the film thus direct us to several rather different genres and sub-genres, and these coexist in a complex fusion. What the film 'means' to us is the sense that we make of this intersection of distinct points of reference.

FIGURES OF GENRE

The cues that alert us to what a text is doing are references to the text's generic frame, and they work by either explicit or implicit invocation of the structures and themes that we characteristically associate with that frame. Texts may also refer to other genres, either as something external to them, or by embedding them within their own overarching generic structure, as in the example, say, of a legal document embedded in a novel, or by means of cues which invoke different genres, in such a way that there is a tension between them.

We could think of these references as transactions or negotiations between writer and reader, where 'writer' and 'reader' are understood as positions rather than, directly, persons. They are the ways in which texts seek to situate themselves rhetorically, to define and delimit their uptake by a reader – and, conversely, they are the ways in which readers make sense of these markers, and indeed notice them and respond to them in the first place. Textual cues are thus **metacommunications**, aspects of the text which somehow stand out as being also, reflexively, *about* the text and how to use it. They may stand out in very obvious ways, like the laugh track in a television sitcom or the moral appended to a fable; or they may merely be elements which seem to take on a particular weight in our reading, and so to be indicative of what kind of thing this is. What we notice reinforces our sense of the kind of thing we're reading, and this in turn activates for us the relevant ranges of information that we need in order to read it well. And part of this information has to do with the speech situation in which relations of reading are being negotiated.

I wrote in Chapter 1 that genres have to do with the strategic work accomplished by texts in particular circumstances; in Carolyn Miller's terms, genres are 'typified rhetorical actions based in recurrent situations' (Miller 1994a: 31). Ross Chambers demonstrates this rhetorical work by talking about how the 'point' of a story may vary when it is told in different situations: his example is of 'a "faggot" joke told by gay people among themselves, by straight people among themselves, by a straight person to a gay person and even, just conceivably, by a gay person to a straight person. In each of these cases, the significance of the story is determined less by its actual content than by the point of its being told, that is, the relationships mediated by the act of narration' (Chambers 1984: 3). The story is not just a thing said but is also an act of enunciation which intervenes in, and in part constructs, a social relationship.

Not all texts work in such a direct way, however. Any text communicated to an *unknown* audience, whether it be a complex aesthetic text or an advertisement, a chain letter or a message in a bottle, must negotiate its relationship with strangers whose response it cannot fully gauge in advance. It must therefore strengthen those reflexive cues by which it signals its strategic intentions, and one of the ways it may do this is by means of an internal 'modelling' of the whole text. Literary narrative, Chambers argues, may thus include 'as part of its self-reference system specific indications of the narrative situation appropriate to it' (Chambers 1984: 4): little models of speaker–hearer relations, figures of aesthetic communication. In more general terms, this means a reflexive modelling of the genre in which the text is working and of the forms of authority and plausibility which form the basis for its proposed contract with the reader.

Yet such models may be misleading or ambiguous, not least because complex aesthetic texts, in particular, are rarely contained by the limits of a single genre. I want to conclude this chapter with an extended reading of a text – Goethe's 1809 novel *Die Wahlverwandtschaften*, usually translated into English as *Elective Affinities* – which does include such a reflexive generic model within it, but which actually works out a more complicated relationship with the genres it performs.

The story of the novel is simply told: a wealthy baron, Eduard, has married Charlotte after both have had intervening marriages in the time since they first knew and loved each other. Into their world they invite Eduard's friend, the Captain, and then Charlotte's niece, Ottilie. Eduard and Ottilie fall in love; so too, in a more restrained way, do Charlotte and the Captain. When things come to a crisis Eduard leaves home and eventually goes to war as a soldier. In the meantime a child is born to Charlotte and Eduard. Eduard eventually returns; the child is accidentally drowned while in Ottilie's care; Ottilie renounces Eduard, stops eating, and eventually dies; and Eduard shortly follows her to the grave.

This story is told in an even more schematic form by Eduard and the Captain when they are talking to Charlotte about the notion of affinities between chemical elements. Each element, they explain, has an adherence to itself and a relation of attraction or antipathy towards other elements; yet through the mediation of a third element, antipathetic elements may be made to combine. When elements separate from an existing union in order to recombine in this way, one can talk of an 'elective affinity', a relationship that is at once given in the order of things and yet in some sense 'chosen'; and when a fourth element is introduced, to pair with the 'divorced' element, then

> one can actually demonstrate attraction and relatedness, this as it
> were crosswise parting and uniting: where four entities, previously

joined together in two pairs, are brought into contact, abandon their previous union, and join together afresh. In this relinquishment and seizing, in this fleeing and seeking, one can really believe one is witnessing a higher determination; one credits such entities with a species of will and choice, and regards the technical term 'elective affinities' as entirely justified.

(Goethe 1971: 55)

The two men then illustrate this process with letters of the alphabet:

Imagine an A intimately united with a B, so that no force is able to sunder them; imagine a C likewise related to a D; now bring the two couples into contact: A will throw itself at D, C at B, without our being able to say which first deserted its partner, which first embraced the other's partner.

(Goethe 1971: 56)

Not only is this, in a nutshell, the story of the adulterous liaison at the heart of the novel, it also exemplifies – and calls attention to – one of the book's narrative strategies, the reduction of human relationships to formal patterning. Walter Benjamin comments, in his essay on the novel, on its 'parsimony of name-giving' and the peculiar 'namelessness' of the characters (Benjamin 1996: 303). In a sense, they all have the same name: Eduard's birth name is the four-letter palindrome 'Otto', but he has relinquished it in favour of his childhood friend, the Captain, whose name it is too. The German name 'Charlotte' is often abbreviated to 'Lotte'; the second female character is Ottilie, and the child is – of course – called Otto. The other, minor characters in the book are called either by their title – 'the Count', 'the architect', 'the schoolteacher' – or by a surname, Mittler ('mediator'), which is an allegory of their character. At one level, then, the world of social differentiations is subordinated to another where identities are transformed or exchanged just as letters are rearranged in a shifting equation. As the plot develops, first Eduard and Charlotte discuss the possibility that their closed relationship will be disrupted by the introduction of a third and then a fourth term; then Eduard and the Captain are drawn to each other and Charlotte is excluded; then the fourth term, Ottilie, is introduced into the equation and is paired first with Charlotte and then with Eduard; then Eduard and Charlotte, each in love with one of the outsiders, make love to each other in a union which is physically conjugal but emotionally adulterous; and finally the child is born bearing the features not of its genetic parents but of the other partners at the lovemaking, the Captain and Ottilie.

In thematic terms, this formal patterning works on a number of different levels, each of which is richly organised through sets of symbolic oppositions. The play of chemical or human elements works through processes of splitting and uniting; the older term for chemist, cited in the novel, is *Scheidekünstler*, 'artist in division', a term which plays on the word for divorce, *Scheidung*, and on the notion of art as a process of bringing things together (as does metaphor) but also as a kind of violence of the imagination. In its strongest sense, formal pattern is dehumanising, belongs to the realm of the demonic. Eduard and Ottilie's relationship works primarily at this level: each gets headaches on, respectively, the right and left side; Ottilie responds strongly to magnetism and to the pull of mineral deposits beneath the earth; when she copies a document her handwriting gradually becomes identical to Eduard's; even when she has moved into silence,

> [she and Eduard] exerted, as before, an indescribable, almost magical attraction upon one another. They lived beneath one roof, but even when they were not actually thinking about one another, when they were involved with other things, driven hither and thither by society, they still drew closer together. If they found themselves in the same room, it was not long before they were standing or sitting side by side. Only the closest proximity to one another could make them tranquil and calm of mind, but then they were altogether tranquil. ... Then they were not two people, they were one person.
>
> (Goethe 1971: 286)

Charlotte and the Captain, by contrast, are capable of moral restraint and self-sacrifice. When, in a boat on the lake, the Captain is carried away and kisses Charlotte, she only 'almost' returns his kiss, and in then deciding that they must renounce each other they exercise a rationality and a capacity for differentiation which is alien to the compulsive love of Ottilie and Eduard.

The world of the demonic, of the 'monstrous forces' (Goethe 1971: 274) that drive the latter couple, is a world of attraction and antipathy at a level deeper than the moral and the social. It is a world of random patterning, the quasi-chemical 'relationships' (or 'affinities') which are beyond human control but which nevertheless seem like 'choices'; a world of natural forces, of fate and of the omens in which Eduard so superstitiously trusts, of poetry and metaphor, and ultimately of death. This world is dominated by the symbolism of water – the 'uncertain element' (Goethe 1971: 110), the 'faithless intractable element' (Goethe 1971: 262) in which the child is drowned. But it is also the world of the imagination – a deeply ambivalent concept in this book because of its transcendence of human limits and human morality, as in the extraordinary moment of conjugal adultery, when,

> in the lamplit twilight inner inclination at once asserted its rights, imagination [*die Einbildungskraft*] at once asserted its rights over reality. Eduard held Ottilie in his arms. The Captain hovered back and forth before the soul of Charlotte. The absent and the present were in a miraculous way entwined, seductively and blissfully, each with the other.
>
> (Goethe 1971: 106)

The counter-world of social and moral order, by contrast, is dominated by the metaphor of gardening and the discourse of 'improvement' (that is, the landscaping of the estate and the renovation of the village, the graveyard, and the chapel), and is supported by several secondary discourses to do with education and with moral conduct. It is a language strikingly close to that of Jane Austen's *Mansfield Park*. Here the understanding is that form cannot be imposed on the natural world, but must emerge organically from it: as Charlotte puts it, 'if we are to enjoy our gardens they have to look like open country; there should be no evidence of art or constraint' (Goethe 1971: 218). In this world, marriage is crucial to social order, as is continuity with the past and its marking by due ceremonial.

These thematic patterns are worked out, then, on a number of different levels, opposing nature to art, the metaphoric to the literal, passion to the social order, the limitless to social measure. Yet, as Tanner points out:

> in reading the book we should beware of thinking that we are inter-
> preting a dimension of meaning of which the characters are unaware.
> It is the other way around. We become aware of the dimension of mean-
> ing that they inhabit. We are not interpreters; rather we are forced into
> a realisation of the hermeneutics within which the characters move
> and have their being. What we might, as readers, consider too obvi-
> ous, too significant, is a projection of the signifiers by which the char-
> acters define their existence and beyond which they cannot see.
>
> (Tanner 1979: 179–80)

But if the novel's characters precede and represent us in elaborating this hermeneutics, these ways of making sense of the world, their activity is in turn the effect of a particular way of ordering symbols along multiple metaphoric levels, and thus of a particular form of readability built into the book's texture in order to guide us through it. It is the effect of the conventions of interpretability given by a particular generic frame.

The book is subtitled 'a novel', *ein Roman*. Yet there are reasons for thinking that it might be written in accordance with more specific conventions. One of them is the existence of an embedded novella in Part Two, Chapter Ten. *Die wunderlichen Nachbarskinder: Novelle* ('The Wayward Young Neighbours: A Novella') is a tale told by the companion of a visiting English lord, the man who has subjected Ottilie to experiments with magnetism. It tells the story of two children who grow up displaying a strong antipathy towards each other. The boy goes away, the girl becomes engaged to someone else. When the boy returns during the engagement festivities, however, the girl realises that her feelings towards him have changed; on a boating expedition she throws herself into the water in order to 'wed herself eternally to his imagination and remorse' (Goethe 1971: 240–1). The boy saves her and they declare their love for each other, having made their way 'from water to earth, from death to life, from the family circle to the wilderness, from despair to rapture, from indifference to passionate affection, and all in a moment' (Goethe 1971: 243). Dressed in borrowed wedding clothes, they then seek their parents' blessing.

Clearly, this story takes up some of the novel's central themes: the play of antipathy and attraction, the transformative role of water which here leads from death to life rather than from life to death; the embedded novella is the comic version of the novel's tragedy, in the sense that it concludes with the unity of discordant elements and with the wedding of the young lovers. Yet it also models the novel's narrative form. The genre of the novella – a genre elaborated in a very particular way in eighteenth-century Germany, not least by Goethe – requires brevity and concision, a unity of action like that of drama, the subordination of character psychology to plot, a sense of inevitability, and the presence of a narrative voice. Now, with the exception of brevity, all of these structural features characterise *Elective Affinities*, and indeed it is in part the prompt provided by this novella that reminds us that the novel does have a narrator, who betrays his presence only by an occasional phrase, as when he speaks of the selection that 'we' have made from the 'beloved' pages [*ihrer liebenswürdigen Blätter*] of Ottilie's journal (Goethe 1971: 163). We are reminded, that is to say, that this story is told by someone, from a certain moral perspective that we are not necessarily meant to share. Yet at the same time the novella form which helps structure the novel imposes a kind of externality on the way we apprehend the characters, a refusal of introspection which is reinforced by that 'namelessness' of the central figures. Benjamin writes that Goethe 'ennobles (so to speak) the form of the novel through that of the novella' by means of his 'refusal to summon the reader's sympathy into the centre of the action itself'; and he adds:

> if the novel, like a maelstrom, draws the reader irresistibly into its interior, the novella strives toward distance, pushing every living creature out of its magic circle. In this way, despite its breadth, *Elective Affinities* has remained novella-like. In its effectiveness of expression, it is not superior to the actual novella contained in it. In it, a boundary form has been created, and by virtue of this fact it stands further removed from other novels than those novels stand from one another.
>
> (Benjamin 1996: 330)

It is the visible exertion of narrative control, too, that results in the book's strong sense of formal patterning, akin perhaps to the structure of Henry James's *The Golden Bowl* (1904) with its playing out of the permutations of the relations between the four main characters; or, in a very different way, imagined by the novelist Morelli in Cortazar's *Hopscotch* (first published in Spanish in 1963) as a series of interactions between characters without 'psychology' and resembling those of 'chemistry, electromagnetism, the secret flow of living matter' (Cortazar 1966: 361–2). For Hillis Miller the novel's 'basic paradigm' is that 'human relations are like the substitutions in metaphorical expressions' (Miller 1992: 171). That dimension of the novel which has to do with the exploration of formal pattern parallels the thematic strand concerned with the necessity imposed by the contingent play of natural forces as they shift from one pattern of attraction and antipathy to another, and with the complicity of art in this process.

Yet the novella is not the only internalised model of the overall text. Another, and perhaps equally powerful, embedded genre is the intimate journals of Ottilie. In one sense what these do is break the relentlessly external perspective of the narrative in order to convey a sense of the inwardness of character: this is a first-person narrative, a voice speaking in its own right. In another sense, of course, there is nothing particularly 'personal' about these journals: Ottilie confides no secrets, and they are largely, it seems, transcriptions from other texts of pious and often platitudinous moral aphorisms. Indeed, Benjamin argues that what is striking about the 'mute notations' of the journal entries is precisely their lack of interiority, since Ottilie moves in a mythic rather than a moral sphere (Benjamin 1996: 337–8): she is driven by fate rather than by deliberation and decision. Hillis Miller writes of the way in which Ottilie *fails* to complete the metaphorical *ratio* in which she is the fourth but asymmetrical term: she 'ruins the ratio' because 'she is an unidentifiable final term, silent or absent'; she 'cannot be worked into a logical and transparent system of substitutions and displacements' (Miller 1992: 212, 221). Yet the point nevertheless holds that what speaks to us here is a purely private voice, one that escapes the omniscience of the narrator and releases us from his hold. And this voice, speaking to us of morality, piety, and decorum, is at the same time the voice of that character above all in the novel who is given over to fate, to silence, and to the 'monstrous forces' of the natural world.

Novel, novella, and journal correspond to different modes of organisation of symbolic material. The form of this novel itself, I suggest, is only in part 'novella-like'; it is, rather, an encompassing form, incorporating and making direct use of a range of expressive possibilities but not reducible to any one of them. The core of its generic structure is its weaving together of the discursive range of the different genres it absorbs and transforms. To interpret any complex text of this kind is not merely an activity of deciphering textually inscribed meanings; it is, as well and more importantly, the act of understanding how those meanings are organised by high-level discursive structures such as those of genre, and of how the text may reflexively figure them.

6

SYSTEM AND HISTORY

GENRE SYSTEMS

Language, including the 'languages' of film or painting or music, makes possible the generation of a potentially infinite number of unique utterances. In practice, however, the utterances that we produce tend to look similar in some but not every respect to other utterances; they are partial repetitions of a kind. This is to say that language is systemically organised not only at the level of phonetics or syntax but also at the level of use. The production of speech or writing is not a free flow of utterances but is shaped and constrained by the norms of rhetorical appropriateness that I have called genre. As Todorov puts it, 'any verbal property, optional at the level of language, may be made obligatory in discourse; the choice a society makes among all the possible codifications of discourse determines what is called its *system of genres*' (Todorov 1990: 10).

It is important to be clear, however, about the sense in which the word 'system' can be used here. The 'system of genres' is neither closed nor stable, and indeed we should perhaps not speak of a single system. Rather, we could posit that there are sets of genre systems organised by domain, those of film or television or literature or architecture, for example; that they are open-ended; and that they are more or less constantly shifting and evolving. Indeed, it may be the case that there is not, or no longer, a single system of film genres or literary genres; there may only be relatively disconnected sub-systems representing relatively disconnected organisations of value. If we can still speak of system, it is because genres are not positive classes, defined only by their salient features, but are defined in relational terms which distinguish these features according to their place and function: a television advertisement is not a programme, and has a range of markers such as length, speed of cutting, production values, and commercial punch-line that differentiate it from programme segments; a newspaper editorial is differentially defined in relation to news stories or opinion columns; the milonga is and is not the same kind of musical form as the tango. We can identify a genre because we are at some level aware of other genres that it is not, and it is this relationship that is systemic.

At the same time, the concept of system is a way of talking about the formal or informal hierarchies of value that operate in any period, such that the epic will be seen to outrank the ode, or the brand-name Hollywood art movie (a David Lynch, a Tarantino, a Coen brothers, say) outranks an anonymous teen movie. At their most formal, such systems amount to a kind of policing: the neoclassical criticism of the late seventeenth and early eighteenth centuries worked in this way to establish rigid norms which corresponded to and enforced a hierarchy of the literary genres; and Bann has analysed the hierarchy established in the early nineteenth century by the French Academy, working through the Salon jury which controlled exhibitions, between two broad genres of painting: the *genre historique*, comprising Biblical, historical, and mythological subjects, and the *genre secondaire*, comprising 'inferior subject matter such as landscape, as well as works whose relatively small scale debarred them from being considered true history paintings' (Bann 2003: 501). This ranking was enforced through the academicians' control of the education of young artists and of the subjects offered for competition in the prestigious Prix de Rome. Bann argues, however, that it is precisely the strictness of this policing of public display that opens the way for the Modernist break with the traditions of the Academy towards the end of the century, and so for the eventual formation of an alternative system.

Let me draw an analogy to try to clarify the sense in which genres of representation may be said to form a system. The analogy is with the different kinds of shop that make up the contemporary order of retailing. I don't mean actual shops, which are self-contained and fixed in place, but the *kinds* of shop that we know and regularly use, and on the basis of which we distinguish actual shops.

The first feature of shops to which I want to draw attention is that they are more or less specialised, and that we know how to use them according to these specialisations: we buy meat from the butcher, not from the baker. But within these specialisations there are some categories that are central to the shop's function (books, for the bookshop) and others that are more marginal (compact discs, stationery, or coffee). This is to say that shops tend to sell a range of goods which are clustered around a semantic core ('bread', 'fresh produce', 'financial services', 'women's clothing'), and others which are further away from this core. At the margins there may be considerable overlap.

Shops differ in the degree to which this core category is well-defined. Some have very precise core functions: a women's clothing boutique doesn't necessarily sell underwear or pyjamas, but will usually sell dresses, blouses, jackets, and so on, and may or may not sell overcoats and accessories such as handbags or belts. A liquor store always sells spirits, beer, and wine, and may or may not sell cigarettes or cigars. A delicatessen sells preserved meats, cheeses, biscuits, and preserves: foods which are 'fine' rather than the staples that one might buy in the grocer's shop. An electrical shop sells major and minor electrical appliances, as well as goods which are more accurately thought of as 'electronic', and perhaps including computers and digital cameras which one could also find in specialist computer or photography shops.

Other shops have a much less clearly defined core. The hardware shop, which used to sell things defined as being made of metal ('hard'), now sells 'things for the maintenance of the home' (tools, equipment for doing repairs), which may or may not be metallic; but it will not sell the contents of the home, such as furniture; it will sell curtain railings and pelmets but not the curtains themselves; it may sell garden tools or fertilisers, but probably not plants or flowers. And it is likely to sell a huge range of miscellaneous objects (tape, ironing boards, lighter fluid, candles) which have in common only that they are of use in the home.

Some shops are more miscellaneous still. The prototype is perhaps the small corner shop (or 'general store' or 'convenience store' or 'mixed business'), historically derived from the older grocery and selling milk, bread, newspapers, groceries, fruit and vegetables, and perhaps some hardware; in resort towns, such shops will also sell fishing or camping or sporting gear. Other examples would be the gift shop, where the category 'gift' mixes together and subsumes other categories such as luxury food, clothing, furniture, or knick-knacks; and the discount shop, pound shop, or nickel-and-dime store, which similarly brings together clothing, minor electrical goods, stationery, cosmetics, and so on.

These classes of shop are of course culturally specific. In the United States the drugstore has so differentiated itself from the older pharmacy, selling prepared medications, that it is now more like a general purpose store, selling a range of foodstuffs, cheap clothing, cosmetics, perhaps food and drink, and quite possibly no 'drugs' at all other than alcohol and nicotine. In some countries one buys stamps from the Post Office; in many European countries one buys them from the tobacconist, who may also sell lottery tickets. Stationery is sometimes sold in a stationery shop, sometimes in a newsagent's shop; and in some countries there is no such class of shop as the newsagency. And yet the point is that we know where to go to buy what we need; or, if we're living in strange parts, we quickly find out.

This varying and unstable division of functions between shops, then, is something like the distinction between genres, and indeed one could, at a stretch, talk about 'genres' of shop. As with the genres of talk or of writing or of film or television, the division between kinds of shop is conventional and culturally specific, and has real effects on our actions. It channels our behaviour, sending us here for some purchases, there for others, according to an understanding that all competent members of the community possess. This understanding is culturally learned: children's books teach them about the butcher, the baker, and the candlestick maker. It involves differential forms of decoration and signage which signal the shop's function: in an older world these would be the barber's pole or the cigar-store Indian; today, it would be distinctive forms of naming, design and display schemes. It involves a distinction between shops and cognate categories such as banks or restaurants, although takeaway restaurants blur one of these borders. And it is embedded in institutional and economic structures such as rental agreements in shopping malls, zoning and licensing regulations, chains of distribution by wholesalers, and franchising contracts.

Because they are culturally specific, however, these understandings are also fluid and changeable: the kinds of shop evolve, the mix of categories is constantly changing. New genres of shop, new retailing structures, evolve. Currently I notice the emergence of single-brand shops (Sony, Occitane), although these have existed in some form, in tailors' shops, for example, for a long time. The pharmacy, as I mentioned, has evolved, at different speeds in different countries, from selling prepared medicinal drugs to selling proprietary non-medicinal products, particularly cosmetics. The haberdashery has now almost completely disappeared. Most powerfully, the department store and the supermarket have displaced and recombined older, cellular forms in powerful new conglomerations, where clusters of the older kinds of shop have been subsumed within the new form while still often retaining their separate identity: the delicatessen counter, the clothing department, and single-brand areas within it. Indeed, new functions continue to evolve: my supermarket will now sell me home loans, car insurance, or even after-school tutoring for my children.

The analogy, then, is manifold: shops, like genres, are cultural forms, dynamic and historically fluid, and guiding people's behaviour; they are learned, and they are culturally specific; they are rooted in institutional infrastructures; they classify objects in ways that are sometimes precise, sometimes fuzzy, but always sharper at the core than at the edges; and they belong to a system of kinds, and are meaningful only in terms of the shifting differences between them.

SYNCHRONY AND DIACHRONY

At the time of writing this book the *Genreflecting* website at www.genre-flecting.com (current 20.3.2005), designed primarily as a guide for librarians and booksellers, contains a sketch of two distinct literary genre systems. The first is that of what the site calls 'genre-specific fiction', on the assumption that the popular genres are in some sense more 'generic' than 'literary fiction'. This system is made up of the following:

Adventure/Suspense
Christian Fiction
Crime and True Crime
Fantasy
Historical
Horror
Mystery and Detection
Romance
Science Fiction
Western

Romance – to take just one of these – is defined, following Ramsdell (1999), as 'a love story in which the central focus is on the development and satisfactory resolution of the love relationship between the two main characters, written in such a way as to provide the reader with some degree of vicarious emotional participation in the courtship process', and it is in turn said to be made up of the following system of sub-genres:

Contemporary
> (Basic Contemporary Romance, Women's Romantic Fiction, Soap Opera, Glitz and Glamour, Contemporary Americana)

Romantic Mysteries
> (Gothic, Romantic Suspense)

Historical Romance
> (Historical Novels, Romantic Historicals, Period Romance, Sensual Historical and Sweet/Savage Romance, Western, Period Americana)

Regency Romance
> (really a sub-genre of historical romance, but large enough to warrant its own category)

Alternative Reality Romance
> (Fantasy, Futuristic, Paranormal, Time Travel)

Sagas

Gay and Lesbian Romance

Inspirational Romance

Ethnic/Multicultural Romance

The second major system defined by the site is entitled 'Beyond Genres', and is for those whose 'taste runs along more literary lines'. It is made up of these genres:

African American
Children's Fiction
Contemporary Mainstream
Easy Reads
Native American
Recreational Nonfiction
Teen Fiction
Transborder (Latino)
Women's Fiction
Jewish American Fiction

However idiosyncratic these categories may appear, and however specific to the United States, they clearly reflect both market distinctions and categories with which readers identify in deciding what to read. More importantly for my purposes, the division of the field (roughly between 'popular' and 'literary' genres) is an indication of a systemic hierarchy of value that actually exists for a large group of contemporary readers. It throws an interesting light on the institutional structures by which such hierarchies are created and maintained.

Writing about the eighteenth-century Russian ode, Tynianov notes that the assignment of a text to a genre takes place only in relation to a particular generic system. What this means is that 'if a work is torn from the context of a given literary system, and transposed into another, its colouring changes, it acquires other features, it enters another genre and loses its own genre, and in other words, its function becomes different' (Tynianov 2003: 565). This implication of the concept of system has been of central importance to the Russian Formalists, particularly to Tynianov, since it requires us to understand that texts do not have an identity with themselves: their forms of coherence and the functions they perform change as the system itself changes, and this systemic change in turn shifts the balance between the genres. What we think of as the 'same' text will change as it passes from one system to another, either in its passage through time, and thus its introduction into very different contexts, or in its translation into other systems. Thus when the Shakespearean texts are read within the framework of European romanticism, they come to signify the barbaric lawlessness of a more vital culture, and are placed on the same shelf as the mythical Celtic poet Ossian. When Charles Dickens's *David Copperfield* is rewritten (that is, re-read) by Dostoevsky's *Crime and Punishment*, or his *Bleak House* by Kafka's *The Trial*, the Dickens novels become something quite different from what they were: less cosy, more metaphysical in their implications. Western television advertisements broadcast into Soviet-era Eastern Europe became a promise of capitalist plenty rather than a merely commercial form.

Conversely, the continuity of a generic name may disguise real discontinuities in its content as it passes from one system to another. Here the classic case is perhaps that of the elegy. In ancient Greece and Rome the genre is defined metrically, by its use of the elegiac distich (the *elegeion*), a line of six dactylic feet followed by a broken pentameter of twice two-and-a-half feet built around a sharp caesura:

In the hexameter rises the fountain's silvery column,
In the pentameter aye falling in melody back –

– a line which, as Potts puts it, 'offers an opportunity for many sorts of doubling phrase to secure emphasis by repetition or contrast' (Potts 1967: 13). Its thematic content varies considerably, including exhortations to battle, commemoration of the dead, dedications at shrines, epigrams and political satire, and love poems. Although it was later linked to the *elegeia* or *elegos*, the lament for the dead, this was never its exclusive function, and in Roman poetry, when it flares into new existence for the 50-odd years before the birth of Christ, the elegy has a very specific life as a kind of sardonic love poem. In the work of Gallus, Tibullus, Propertius, and Ovid it draws on the Hellenistic lyric and on the New Comedy plot of the dissolute young man subjected to the whims of his courtesan mistress and in conflict with the older husband or protector; but its first-person speaker and the mode of ironic consciousness it embodies, together with its subversion of the values of Republican virtue, separate it quite dramatically from its predecessors (Miller 2004: 4).

With the rise of the European vernacular literatures the metrical form of the elegiac distich drops away as the defining feature of the genre, to be replaced by a thematic definition having to do with mourning. In English, this content has particular prominence in the funeral elegy of the seventeenth century, and indeed Pigman argues that its popularity corresponds to a shift in attitudes towards mourning, in which 'an ideal of personal expression of grief begins to replace critical self-restraint' (Pigman 1985: 3). From this shift in the seventeenth century we can trace another in the eighteenth, in which the 'graveyard poetry' of Young's 'Night Thoughts' (1742), Blair's 'The Grave' (1743), and Gray's 'Elegy Written in a Country Churchyard' (1751), 'by generalising the subject-matter of the elegy and freeing it from the confines of merely occasional verse, bridged the transition between the elegy proper ... and the melancholy of nascent Romanticism both in England and on the continent' (Draper 1967: 4). What Draper maps here is a shift from the *genre* of the elegy to the elegiac *mode*. Morton Bloomfield, too, differentiates them, saying that 'in English, the elegiac mode is largely, though not exclusively, the creation of the Romantic movement, and it has flourished from about 1750 to today, when it has perhaps become the predominant mode and mood of lyric poetry'; it 'is not a genre but a mode of approaching reality' (Bloomfield 1986: 148). Mode here is a matter of tone – of reflective melancholy or sadness – whereas the elegy as a genre remains more specifically concerned with the act of mourning a particular person.

At any one time, a genre such as the elegy is a dynamic member of a broader economy of genres – that is, of a set of forms which are differentially related to each other. The funeral elegy of the seventeenth century is defined by its relation to the epitaph, the anniversary, and the epicede or funeral ode, a group of genres addressing an occasion of mourning and having the function of commemoration. At the same time, this group is a component of the broader system of poetic genres, and beyond that to the economy of literary genres (that is, of all the forms of writing) as a whole: the elegy is both like and unlike the funeral sermon, for example. These economies, these systems of differential relations, are worked out very differently in different periods. Take, for example, Frank O'Hara's elegy 'For James Dean', written in September 1955 in the week following the actor's death. Invoking the gods who have indulged in 'your whim / of ending him', the speaker who begs peace for the 'young actor' is also his spirit:

Men cry from the grave while they still live
and now I am this dead man's voice,
stammering, a little in the earth.

(O'Hara 1974: 98)

Yet this elegy is also a poem of denunciation of one of the dominant institutions of O'Hara's time, just as Milton's 'Lycidas' combines mourning with denunciation of the corruption of the church: attacking the machinations of the film industry, the poem is the negative counterpart of O'Hara's upbeat ode 'To the Film Industry in Crisis' (1955) with its address not to the literary periodical nor the experimental theatre nor to 'Grand Opera, obvious as an ear (though you / are close to my heart)' but to 'you, Motion Picture Industry, / it's you I love!' (O'Hara 1974: 99). This is to say that the economy of genres invoked by O'Hara's elegy defines a meaningful relationship between literature, here in the knowingly archaic form of a prayer to the gods, and the movies, particularly the popular genres that O'Hara's camp sensibility embraces. Even more traditional, less ironically archaising elegies, like Auden's poems on the death of Yeats and Freud, with their respective reminiscences of Blake and Horace, still refer indirectly to other parts of the economy of literary and non-literary genres, and are internally shaped by it.

Because of its shifting historical content, and thus because of its shifting relation to other genres within particular historical economies of genre, the elegy cannot be said to have a fixed set of characteristics which is peculiar to it. It is a different kind of thing at different times. Yet many critics have tried to establish such a core function which would characterise all representatives of the genre at all times, and allow us to posit a continuity between its earliest and its most recent forms. Fowler notes that Scaliger suggests 'that the matter of love elegy is connected with that of funeral elegy by the lover's "death" ' (Fowler 1982: 136). Farrell, seeking to establish a commonality between the Latin love elegy and the elegy of lamentation, makes a similar, if perhaps more qualified, suggestion:

> The elegists regularly brood on death, labeling their genre a poetry of
> lament. Of course, what they normally lament is not anyone's death,
> but the fact that they themselves are living out their lives as slaves to
> love. But because the two notions of 'love' and 'death' share in the
> idea of 'lament', they are treated as if they were perfectly compatible,
> even equivalent, constituents of the genre.
>
> (Farrell 2003: 398)

For Bloomfield the elegy is essentially an epideictic genre: a genre to
do with praise and blame, but particularly with the latter, since
' "praise" is the crucial and unifying notion, which brings together spir-
ited military and love poems with lamentations for the dead'
(Bloomfield 1986: 155). And for Sacks, the rhetorical force of elegy as
an acting-out of the work of mourning links its function as 'a poem of
mortal loss and consolation' (Sacks 1985: 3) to the earliest associations
of the elegiac flute song with grief and lament.

All of these answers seem to me to be projections from a contemporary understanding to that of other periods: they look for a continuity
and a permanence which it is not in the nature of genres to offer. They
make the same category mistake as Etiemble does when he calls for 'a
systematic study of the novels produced by civilisations far removed
from our own' in order to 'help us demonstrate on the one hand the
invariants of the genre "novel" ', i.e., those elements without which
there is no novel, and on the other hand those characteristics of the
genre which arise more or less arbitrarily from the historical circumstances' (Etiemble 1962: 206). Citing this sentence, Beebee comments:
'It is impossible to separate the historically contingent from the acci-
dental if one already decides *a priori* that *roman*, *novela*, *romance*, novel,
and *monogotari* all refer to the same essence' (Beebee 1994: 125). Genres
have no essence: they have historically changing use values.

The novel is a useful case study here, because its most powerful theorists, those who have achieved the most intense illumination of the expressive capacities of the genre, have all bought their insights at the price of an
essentialisation of those capacities; they have removed the novel from its
full historicity in order to grasp an unchanging core of novelness.
Georg Lukács's *Theory of the Novel* (1916) seems, indeed, to locate historical transformation at the heart of the novel form, taking as its start-

ing point the coincidence of the structural categories of the novel with those of the modern world. As late as 1952, Lukács reaffirms, in an approving summary of Hegel's theory of genre, his belief in the organic connection between the institution of genre and history:

> The forms of the artistic genres are not arbitrary. On the contrary, they grow out of the concrete determinacy of the particular social and historical conditions. Their character, their peculiarity is determined by their capacity to give expression to the essential features of the given socio-historical phase. Hence the different genres arise at particular stages of historical development, they change their character radically (the epic is transformed into the novel), sometimes they disappear completely, and sometimes in the course of history they rise to the surface again with modifications.
>
> (Lukács 1969: 118, my translation)

The literary genre thus stands in an expressive relation to the historical period, but it also expresses the tension between the given historical 'form' (the structure of social life) and an ideal form laid down in the genre as an absolute possibility. The archetype of this ideal form is the epic, and the superiority of the epic to the other genres lies in its capacity for realisation of a fullness of meaning immanent in the world. No other narrative forms can do this, because of their historical estrangement from this plenitude. The novel, in particular, is a necessarily degraded form of epic narrative; in it, the discontinuity between person and social structure becomes a formal component of the text, above all through the use of ironic distance, and 'the immanence of meaning required by the form is attained precisely when the author goes all the way, ruthlessly, towards expressing its absence' (Lukács 1971: 72).

What looks like an embrace of the historicity of formal structures is, then, in the last instance a mythical opposition between two ideal types: a fullness of being in the epic, on the one hand, and on the other the problematic world of lack and estrangement that is the novel. The analysis of formal structures that flows from this opposition – the novel's quest structure, the tension between a meaningful interiority and the senseless world outside, the role of irony, the negative role of time in the novel – postulates a constant form that corresponds to the ontology of modernity, or, in class terms, of the bourgeoisie; it is an invariant and indeed normative form, structured by its negative relation to the epic, and it is perhaps for this reason that, when the novel form mutates, in the work of Dostoevsky, beyond a recognisably 'epic' structure, Lukács characterises it as being no longer truly novelistic.

As I noted earlier, a similar definition of the diversity of the novel form against an invariant counterpart – in this case the monologic structure of poetry – works to **essentialise** the novel in the writings of Bakhtin: the novel comes to work as a *principle* of heteroglossia, of the play of heterogeneous voices, and to the extent that it is split between designating a genre and a mode, denoting 'not only the relatively determinate literary form but also the generalised aura and ethos of that form' (McKeon 1987: 12), it stands as a trans-historical force.

Other accounts of the novel likewise posit a moment of origin that comes to define its core expressive capacity. Ian Watt's definition of the 'formal realism' that he takes to be at the heart of the genre is developed on the one hand in relation to a set of 'external' conditions: the individualistic bourgeois subject form, the growth of mass literacy; and on the other by the genre's separation from, and absorption of, a range of nonliterary genres such as the autobiographical memoir and the intimate letter. The assumption is that the moment of constitution of the genre establishes its essential characteristics, which then continue to be operative in all of the later life of the form. For McKeon the shaping of the novel as 'an early modern cultural instrument' (McKeon 1987: 22) with an 'unrivalled power both to formulate, and to explain, a set of problems that are central to early modern experience' (McKeon 1987: 20) is decisive for its later development precisely because of the persistence of that experience of modernity which the novel helped to initiate. And for Armstrong it is the relation of the novel form to the women's conduct books of the seventeenth and eighteenth centuries that sets it, from Richardson onwards, on its path of actively shaping class relations by displacing them into matters of kinship and of ethical conduct.

But stories of origins need not stop there. They can instead be stories about the intertextual work by which the genre shapes and re-shapes itself in an ongoing and open-ended process. This shaping and re-shaping takes place, of course, in relation to changes elsewhere in the social order, but we should construe this not as a relation of exteriority, in which 'the social' over there has effects on 'literature' over here. Armstrong's exposition of the social force of 'domestic fiction' is exemplary in this respect: the novel, in her account, is directly formative of the world that it describes (Armstrong 1987: 8). It is itself a social relationship, a 'distinctive sphere of social action' (Bennett 1990: 108). If we accept that the form and the function of genres change constantly, then we need to understand both the continuities and the discontinuities in what is designated by a generic label such as 'novel' or 'elegy', as well as the variant constitution of the systems within which genres function as 'particular, socially circumscribed fields of textual uses and effects' (Bennett 1990: 105).

GENRIFICATION

In thinking about genre as a process it becomes important to think about the conditions that sustain it: the institutional forces that govern the determination and distribution of classification and value. Genres emerge and survive because they meet a demand, because they can be materially supported, because there are readers and appropriate conditions of reading (literacy, affordable texts), writers or producers with the means to generate those texts, and institutions to circulate and channel them.

These things are often clearer when we talk about the popular genres of capitalist modernity, since we accept that they are industrially produced, whereas the conditions of production and reception of self-consciously 'aesthetic' texts are often obscured. Here I want to look briefly at Rick Altman's work in *Film/Genre* on the process of what he calls 'genrification' of Hollywood movies, since this goes to the heart of the question of the constitution of genre systems in a complex interplay of institutional factors.

Altman begins by taking exception to the notion that film genres have an objective existence apart from the mechanisms, institutions, and communities that give them life. That *is* their existence, he argues: the processes by which they come and go. Rather than accepting the standard view of genres as having a stable existence, distinct borders, and a regular and predictable development shaped largely by the film industry's calculations of what it is that audiences want, Altman tells a much messier story about the prevalence of genre-mixing in the Hollywood studio system and the slow and uncertain emergence of the substantive genres. By studying the way three genres – the musical, the Western, and the biopic – come into being he is able to show that each of these labels emerges rather late after a period in which the genre term is used only adjectivally: 'Before the Western became a separate genre and a household word, there were such things as Western chase films, Western scenics, Western melodramas, Western romances, Western adventure films, and even Western comedies, Western dramas and Western epics' (Altman 1999: 52).

In the movement by which such adjectival terms acquire the status of nouns ('the Western'), a number of distinct reading positions come into play. Crucially, the studio personnel – producers, accountants, directors, writers – who make the decisions about what kind of movies to make are acting as readers or critics of successful preceding films; their activity is more often than not one of recombination of elements that have worked before, of the '*Out of Africa* meets *Pretty Woman*' type hopefully suggested in the writers' pitches at the beginning of Robert Altman's *The Player*. The process of genrification by which genres emerge as 'industry standards' (Altman 1999: 47) begins with this act of reading and is then consolidated through a broad industry acceptance of it – usually an acceptance that is manifested in imitation and further development – and through a process of public reception in which 'the public, whether self-consciously or not, [has] to become so aware of the structures binding disparate films into a single generic category that the process of viewing would always be filtered through the type concept' (Altman 1999: 53).

Yet this is not the end of the story: change and transformation do not end with the emergence of an identifiable genre, since genre is 'not the permanent *product* of a singular origin, but the temporary *by-product* of an ongoing *process*' (Altman 1999: 54). And while it is the case that genres help structure studio thinking about the making of films, there are several other ways in which the studios, which are usually seen as the primary agents in the development of film genres, actually think in quite different terms. First, it is not the case that studio publicity makes a targeted use of genre concepts, since it tends rather to invoke multiple genres when advertising a new movie in order to attract diverse audiences; and second, studios tend to work with cycles, series, remakes, and sequels, and to publicise films through the figure of the star and sometimes the director, rather than genres, since the former are proprietary rather than sharable. Their preference is for the singularity of the brand name rather than the socially shared form of genre (Altman 1999: 59).

Yet cycles and series tend in turn to become genres, as in the case of the 'woman's film', for example, and the names of stars come to work as a shorthand for the genres in which they work: Bogart and *noir* – if indeed we can think of *noir* as a genre. To say that apparently stable genre names are often retrospective impositions on the messy processes of genrification is merely to say that the categories of genre are subject to constant redefinition. Genre is performed in the activity of reading, and reading has different kinds of authorisation and authority. Film producers are in one sense privileged readers because their readings get turned into new products; but so, in another sense, are audiences, because their responses to movies determine which films will get made, or will not get made, in the future. Critics in turn, as that part of the audience that writes about its reading, exercise a certain institutional power in this often conflictual dialectic of reading positions which shapes the movement and the mutation of genres. Genre takes place in the interplay of readings and of the social force they carry.

TEACHING GENRE

Just as texts are never one-of-a-kind but are always the partial repetitions of a kind, so reading is never simply an individual act, although it is always that. We read and look and listen in ways that are shaped by our experience and our education. These shapings are regular: we read, listen, view, and evaluate in rough accord with the age group, the gender, the ethnicity, the class, and the educational level we belong to, and these variables have different force in different semiotic domains. Age, for example, is the crucial factor in what music we will listen to, and this is then inflected by education and gender; gender and education are the crucial factors governing what we read, and so on (Bennett *et al.* 1999).

The concept I have used in earlier books to describe how these regularities are formed is that of the *regime of reading*. By this I mean simply the shared competencies, norms, and values that govern how we read and the kinds of value we attach to books or films or music (cf. Frow 1986: 185–7 for a somewhat more complex formulation). It is through our learning of the structure of reading regimes that we acquire the background knowledges, and the knowledge of rules of use and relevance, that allow us to respond appropriately to different generic contexts. Any complex society sets in play a number of different regimes which give rise to different patterns of reading: within an overall literary or filmic or visual arts regime we could distinguish between 'popular' and 'educated' regimes, for example, or between 'masculine' and 'feminine' regimes, each of which would yield rather different emphases and different structures of interest. Some genres are more or less exclusive to one regime: the contemporary romance to a 'feminine' regime of reading, say. Others are common to several but are read in rather different ways: *The Simpsons* is both a popular text and a cult text within the more reflexive regime of high culture.

Regimes of reading are structured and sustained by social institutions, some of them very informal, such as talk with friends about what we read or view, or indeed about talk itself; others, such as fan magazines or music websites or book reviews or a school curriculum, are much more formal. Some involve discussion; others, such as library classifications or television time slots or the arrangement of paintings in a museum, are sorting mechanisms which carry implicit orderings of value.

Formal education is one of the most important means by which regimes of reading are inculcated, sustained, and at times contested or qualified. Children learn in school, without ever being explicitly taught it, about the socially sanctioned division of knowledge and the generic differences and differences of value that accompany it; textbooks present themselves, in generically specific ways, as apparently 'autonomous and context-free repositories of factual information' (Haas 1994: 43, cited in Johns 1997: 47); students are taught how to perform such genres as the essay, the multiple-choice exam, the classroom discussion, the debate; and they learn through explicit metacommentary about certain privileged genres such as those of literature and film. What this means is that 'the teaching–learning activities of schools are really curriculum genres: staged, goal-driven, purposive activities, in which students are initiated into ways of working, thinking and dealing with experience' (Christie 1993: 155). Before it is an explicit object of analysis, genre in the school is a medium of instruction.

This should surely be the starting point for all teaching of genre in formal educational institutions. Reflexive analysis of genre involves, in the first instance, a critical reflection on the means and the medium of teaching and the culturally particular division and organisation of knowledge that are carried by these means. Although many of the curriculum genres are cross-disciplinary and carry information primarily about the teaching process, the disciplines themselves tend to be conveyed in generically particular forms, as I indicated in my brief and schematic analysis in Chapter 4 of the genres of philosophy and history. What we can teach is the values built into such genres: what counts as evidence and proof; how space and time, events and their actors, are organised; the structures of authority and plausibility carried by the genre. What can be taught is thus not just a set of formal structures but the backgrounded knowledges that inform and shape them; and not an amorphous body of knowledge or personal experience but the conventional forms that they take in particular contexts.

But the teaching of genre may also take the form of instruction in the practice of genre, especially in writing programmes in secondary and tertiary education. Some of these programmes work as a complement to other kinds of learning, teaching a general academic literacy focused on a few genres like the report and the research essay, and generally envisaging genre as a fixed model to be emulated and reproduced. Others are less functional in their orientation, teaching the open-ended exploration and use of a range of genres, and more concerned with the dynamic nature of textuality than with conformity to a model.

The teaching of genre as a strategically central moment of literacy teaching developed in Australia in the 1990s and shared close parallels with the 'New Rhetoric' in the United States. It represents a response both to the 'traditional literacy pedagogies which stress formal correctness' and to the '**process' pedagogies** of the 1970s 'which stress "natural" learning through "doing" writing' (Cope and Kalantzis 1993: 1). It is the latter, however, that forms the ground against which genre literacy teaching situates itself. The progressivist movement from which 'process' writing is derived is seen as having initiated 'a relativistic theory of cultural and linguistic pluralism' (Cope and Kalantzis 1993: 5) which devalues formal structure and thus impoverishes learning itself: '"Natural" literacy learning ... leads to a pedagogy which encourages students to produce texts in a limited range of genres, mostly person-alised recounts. This is why the texts generated in the process writing classroom ("choose your own topic"; "say what you feel like saying") often end up monotonous and repetitive' (Cope and Kalantzis 1993: 6).

In reaction to this failure (a reaction which they would distinguish, however, from the conservative backlash that calls for a return to 'basics'), the practitioners of genre literacy seek to retain formal **metalanguages** as a way of giving students access to a full range of genres, in all their complexity, and hence to the social purposes of texts-in-use. Genre is a privileged object because of its mediation between social and textual structure: 'Social patterning and textual patterning meet as gen-res' (Cope and Kalantzis 1993: 7). But it is privileged as well in that it moves beyond the divorce that traditional grammar institutes between the structure of the sentence and its purposive use in social situations. Hence the distinctive methodology of genre literacy:

> Starting with the question of purpose, analysis of the text proceeds by looking at the structure of the whole text. Only then does it account for the progress of the whole text in terms of what happens in sen-tences and clauses. ... Genre analysis is concerned primarily with whole texts and their social functions. Sentence and clause analysis is only performed in order to explain the workings of the whole text and how it realises its social purpose.
>
> (Cope and Kalantzis 1993: 10)

Useful as this emphasis on the 'whole text' is, however, as a way of talking about the meaningful and purposive organisation of discourse, it nevertheless rests on two doubtful assumptions: that texts are whole and unitary things, rather than being parts of a broader intertextual process; and that they have or express a singular 'purpose', something akin to the 'intention' of their author. Reid identifies three problems with the assumption of textual unity:

> (1) in so far as generic models do govern particular acts of construct-ing meaning they may be quite different from the traditional models designated by literary taxonomists; (2) several different and even con-tradictory generic elements frequently mingle in a text; (3) since a text

is an exchange of meanings, its genre is to some extent negotiable between author and reader, not simply dictated by the former.

(Reid 1984: 59)

Thus, he continues, the problem with invoking genre as a unifying frame 'is that many texts are formally promiscuous: they fold into themselves a mix of diverse registers without resolving these into a fully cohesive "whole", and indeed the resistance to being generically homogenised may be a large factor in their appeal to readers' (Reid 1984: 61).

These criticisms are part of a broader debate amongst theorists and practitioners of genre literacy about whether genres should be formally modelled, and thus act as norms which students should emulate, or whether teaching should emphasise the dynamic nature of textuality and move beyond a merely instrumental approach to genre (cf. McCarthy and Carter 1994: 28). In a sense, however, this is a false opposition, depending on a prior understanding of genre as a fixed and law-like taxonomy; it assumes that textuality and structure are opposed to each other, rather than seeing textuality as an effect of structure which in turn transforms it. Threadgold suggests that we must think in terms of a dialectic between these two moments, and thus 'teach the interpersonal and textual characteristics of genres, the probabilistic, dynamic aspects of their performance as well as their schematic structures' (Threadgold 1989: 108). We might add that these two moments can also be thought of as stages in a learning process.

Some theorists of genre literacy, in attributing to it a critical and transformative potential, seem to me to overestimate the capacity of the schooling system to effect social change. Kress, for example, argues that the aim of genre literacy teaching has been 'to bring about greater possibilities of access to the resources and the technology of literacy, and, through greater access, to bring about some of the conditions for a redistribution of power in society'; he thus feels that 'a quite revolutionary program might be built on the attempt to give everyone access to literary skills and knowledge in the fullest sense' (Kress 1993: 28–9). Yet he worries, at the same time, that 'the powerful genres of the dominant cultural group(s) will be taught in an unreflecting fashion, as if they were a politically, socially and ideologically neutral set of forms, as a kind of universal commonsense' (Kress 1993: 30). If students are to be integrated into the dominant social groups (that is, to acquire some part of the power that is currently held restrictively) they will surely need to use those 'powerful genres' in the way that the powerful use them; and in any case the idea that 'access to literary skills and knowledge' will by itself transform the social order seems implausible.

Yet, in another sense, the teaching both of a critical knowledge about genres and of the ability to perform a diverse range of genres is central to a critical understanding of and engagement with the social order. Genres carry and organise their culture and fashion our sociality in the broadest sense. As Carolyn Miller puts it:

> What we learn when we learn a genre is not just a pattern of forms or even a method of achieving our own ends. We learn, more importantly, what ends we may have. ... We learn to understand better the situations in which we find ourselves and the potential for failure and success in acting together. As a recurrent, significant action, a genre embodies an aspect of cultural rationality.
>
> (Miller 1994a: 38)

Let me conclude on this note: what we learn, in 'doing' genre (in performing and transforming it), is the values we share or don't share with others and the means with which to challenge or defend them. Through the use of genres we learn who we are, and encounter the limits of our world.

GLOSSARY

Citation   The shifting or displacement of a piece of unmodified text from one context to another.

Class   A group of entities of the same kind, where sameness is measured by a specific criterion defining membership of the class.

Context   Any environment in which a text is situated. Context may itself be textual, or it may be non-textual, and it is delimited according to interpretive need.

Decorum   The codes governing the fit between a stylistic level of utterance and a thematic content. Neoclassical theory thinks of this relation as that between two pre-formed structures (a style and a content); we would now be more likely to think of this as a formative process: the 'humble speech' (*sermo humilis*) of the New Testament, for example, discursively constructs rather than reflects the kind of world it describes.

Dialogic   Bakhtin's term to designate the 'addressivity' that structures all uses of language: that is, the way all language is formed in relation to other (actual or potential) utterances, and thus its sensitivity to the positions and perspectives of other speakers. Some language works to reduce this responsiveness, however, and Bakhtin refers to it as *monologic*, although this is a matter of degree since no language is ever completely free of its relation to other utterances. The concept of dialogism also has ethical and political overtones of openness to other positions and perspectives.

Discourse, discourse community, discursive formation, discursive practice   The concept of discourse refers to three distinct levels of instantiation of language: first, as I use the term in this book, it refers to the organisation of language with reference to the positions of speaking or writing and of reception that it makes possible, the topics and discursive objects it puts in circulation, and the strategic uses to which it may be put in particular kinds of situation; second, it refers to language from the perspective of its *actual* use and in contrast to the system of lexical and grammatical rules (in this sense it could also be termed a **discursive practice**); third, when it is specified as 'a' discourse, it refers either to an organised domain of meaning, or to the actualisation of that domain in spoken or written text (these are the senses it has in Foucault's work). When Foucault speaks of a **discursive formation**, he emphases its heterogeneity: it is made up, in addition to language, of bodies, speakers, organised space, actions, beliefs, norms and values, and institutions. The concept of **discourse community** has been elaborated in the New Rhetoric movement to refer to the fact that organised structures of meaning and value are sustained by groups whose members recognise, use, and renew them.

Dithyramb   An extended Greek choric hymn celebrating the acts of the god Dionysius. Only fragments of the early religious form of the dithyramb survive; the best known exponent of the later, aesthetic form is the poet Pindar, writing in the fifth century before the Christian era.

Enunciation, position of enunciation   The term refers in the first instance to the act of speaking or giving utterance, in contrast to that which is spoken or uttered, and is modelled on the elegant French opposition of the *énonciation* to the *énoncé*. Less literally, it refers to the structure of this act, and to the positions of speaking and receiving a message that organise this structure.

Essentialise   To assume a set of fixed and unchanging characteristics.

Figure, figuration, figurative, figural   A figure is any use of language that deviates from a norm of literal directness. This norm is entirely fictive, but nevertheless productive of our sense of differences in degree between directness and indirectness in language, and of the strategies of translation we use to interpret **figurative** language. The term **figure** may also refer to a modelling of one entity by another, and the **figural** has to do with the model of the human form or person as well as with figures of speech.

Form, formal features The concept of form designates those aspects of a text which are recurrent as opposed to those which are singular. It is a relational concept: every formal feature is at another level an aspect of 'content', and every 'content' can be thought, from another perspective, as a dimension of form. As I use it here, it refers primarily to those elements of a text which recurrently shape the material medium of the text and the 'immaterial' categories of space, time, and enunciative position – that is, the most fundamental categories through which the text is organised.

Frame A metaphor drawn from the material frame surrounding a picture to designate the boundary surrounding and organising any limited piece of information. The frame in this sense gives structure to the delimited text and at the same time situates it in meaningful relation to a context which is other than the text. The frame is thus both a part of the text and other than it, ambiguously mediating and defining an inside and an outside.

Heteroglossia Bakhtin's term for the orientation of language to a multiplicity of other languages. Although it is similar in meaning to **dialogism** (q.v.), the latter tends to refer to the relation of one utterance to another, whereas heteroglossia tends to refer to the responsiveness of an utterance to larger structures such as genres, language varieties and dialects, jargons, styles, and so on.

Horizon of expectations Jauss's term, developed from the phenomenological philosophy of Husserl, to designate the structured set of knowledges and values that form the background understanding for any reception of a text. This background understanding is not merely a resource to be drawn on, but actively structures what we are able and likely to perceive in the reading of a text, and, just as importantly, what is likely to be culturally invisible to us.

Iconography The term designates both knowledge about the conventional meanings of images and their themes, and those conventional meanings themselves, which is the way I use the term here; in this sense it resembles the concept of the literary *topos*.

Implication, implicature In formal logic, implication is a relation between two propositions such that if the first holds, so does the second. The second proposition is said to be logically entailed by the first. Grice's concept of **implicature** refers to the meanings of an utterance that go beyond what is strictly implied by the content of the utterance; it corresponds to what I and other ordinary speakers of English refer to as **implication**.

Information In mathematical information theory, information is a measure of the degree of organisation, complexity, and probability of a message: the greater its probability, the less information it carries. Complex messages are likely to be highly entropic (that is, 'disorganised' in the sense of being highly unpredictable) and thus to have a high information content. Messages with a high degree of redundancy (recurrent patterning), by contrast, will have a low information value. As I use the term in this book, 'information' refers to any organised knowledge about the world.

Institution Any socially established entity carrying a weight of authority because of its duration over time.

Intertextuality The elaboration of a text in relation to other texts. The radical import of the concept in contemporary criticism has to do with its implication that, rather than being self-contained and self-present structures, texts are traces and tracings of otherness, shaped by the repetition and transformation of other texts.

Kairos and ***chronos*** I take these terms from Kermode (1966: 46–50), who uses them to distinguish between the empty succession of moments in passing time (*chronos*) and the fullness of time, the time of significant change or crisis that is *kairos*.

Keying Goffman's term, based on a musical analogy, to indicate a shift or transcription of a behaviour from a primary usage to a secondary usage, such as play or art. He defines it more precisely as 'the set of conventions by which a given activity, one already meaningful in terms of some primary framework, is transformed into something patterned on this activity but seen by the participants to be something quite else' (Goffman 1974: 43–4).

Knowledges Following Foucault's usage, I employ this word in the plural in order to indicate that knowledge does not form a unified totality but is differentiated by conventional divisions into distinct but overlapping spheres.

Language game Wittgenstein's term for certain kinds of organisation of discourse is meant to indicate 'the fact that the *speaking* of language is part of an activity, or of a form of life'. The examples he gives are partly speech acts and partly genres; they include such things as:

Giving orders and obeying them –

Describing the appearance of an object, or giving its measurements –

Constructing an object from a description (a drawing) –

Reporting an event –

Speculating about an event –

Forming and testing a hypothesis –

Presenting the results of an experiment in tables and diagrams –

Making up a story; and reading it –

Play-acting –

Singing catches –

Guessing riddles –

Making a joke; telling it –

Solving a problem in practical arithmetic –

Translating from one language into another –

Asking, thanking, cursing, greeting, playing.

(Wittgenstein 1968: 11–12)

Literature, the literary A relatively recent term, coinciding around the end of the eighteenth century with the autonomisation of art (that is, its shift from systems of patronage to the impersonality of the market), and designating a valued body of secular writings; more narrowly, these writings are restricted to 'imaginative' texts. In a broader sense, the term refers not only to a body of texts but to the social relations that sustain it and the institutional structures in which they are embedded.

Metalanguage, metageneric, metacommunication The prefix 'meta' indicates information which refers from a higher logical level to information at a lower logical level. Metalanguage is language referring to language, and so on.

Modality The indication by a speaker of his or her assessment of the validity of what is said: by the use of such grammatical means as auxiliary verbs or qualifying adverbs, a proposition is characterised as being true, necessary, desirable, possible, known, believed, permissible, and so on. Logicians distinguish between the following kinds of modality: *alethic*, having to do with truth, necessity or possibility; *epistemic*, expressing my knowledge of what I am saying; *doxastic*, expressing my belief; *deontic*, having to do with obligation or permission; and *boulomaeic*, expressing my desires or preferences in relation to the proposition. The tense of the verb is sometimes counted as a form of modality.

Modernity Apparently a period concept, 'modernity' is a way of constructing the distinctiveness of the post-traditional world. It is thus broader than the concept of capitalism, although it is roughly coextensive with it. Its binary construction in relation to the traditional means that the concept tends to impose both a periodising unity and a normative value on the heterogeneous historical materials it incorporates.

Multiplicity As I use it here, the word carries overtones of its Deleuzian meaning of an open-ended plurality which is not reducible to the totality either of the One or of the Many; multiplicity is number without closure.

Neoclassical (theory) The forms of normative poetics that flourished in Europe from about 1650 to the late eighteenth century. Drawing on Aristotle, Horace, Cicero, and Quintilian, such critics as Dryden, Boileau, Batteux, Rapin, Voltaire, Addison, and Johnson sought a systematic understanding of the 'rules' of poetic composition, including an understanding of the rule-governed nature of the literary genres.

New Comedy Comedies of manners and of the complications of love, and performed without a chorus, the New Comedy is represented by the work of the Athenian Menander and the Romans Plautus and Terence.

Old Comedy Represented only by the surviving works of Aristophanes, the Old Comedy of Athens is performed with a chorus, revolves around topical political concerns, and is loosely structured as a form of burlesque and often bawdy slapstick humour.

Ontology The nature of a thing's being, the mode of being which is distinctive of it; an **ontological domain** is any area of being which is in some way circumscribed as distinctive.

Overdetermination Freud develops the concept to describe the logic of complex or multiple causalities: for example the fusion of several different thought-contents in a dream image.

Performative Performative speech acts, as Austin defines them, are those utterances which bring about a state of affairs by virtue of the act of utterance: the words 'I marry you' or 'I declare war', when pronounced under the appropriate circumstances by someone with the authority to perform these acts, bring about a marriage or a state of war. In contemporary theory the concept of the performative often refers more generally to the capacity of language, or other representational media, to constitute the realities they refer to.

Poetics The attempt to construct a systematic account of verbal art forms; by extension, any systematic account of organised textuality of any kind.

Predicate A grammatical term referring to that part of the sentence which says something about the subject of the sentence; a description of the properties of an entity, or of an event occurring in relation to it. In English, predication is performed by a verb phrase in relation to a noun phrase.

Process pedagogies Forms of teaching developed in the 1960s and 1970s which emphasise the need for the learning of writing to occur organically in a process of exploration and self-expression on the part of the student, rather than through the inflexible imposition of a curriculum.

Prototype That member of a class whose properties seem most clearly to exemplify the typical features of the class.

Reflexive Including itself, or having the capacity to include itself, as an object of analysis or reference.

Repetition I use the word here in the sense it has in the work of Deleuze and Derrida, where even the most exact recurrence of an event involves a degree of change because of the temporal and contextual displacement it undergoes.

Representation The meaning of this word has shifted in the course of the twentieth century from designating the secondary imitation of a primary reality, to designating the construction in a signifying medium of a text which carries an effect of reality of some kind. A representation is a text considered in terms of its capacity to produce such an effect, regardless of its relation to any external reality.

Rhetorical Having to do with the interaction between speaker and receiver, or with the effects of an utterance upon an audience

Role Theatrical in origin, the term designates the disjunction between an embodied self and the functions it performs or the positions it occupies.

Russian Formalists A loose grouping of literary scholars in Moscow and St Petersburg who were active between 1915/16 and 1929, when the movement was suppressed. They included Viktor Shklovsky, Roman Jakobson, Boris Eichenbaum, Boris Tomashevsky, and Yuri Tynianov, and were widely influential in seeking to establish a theoretical basis for the formal analysis of literary texts.

Semiotic, semiosis, semiotic medium   **Semiotics** is a science of signs envisaged by Saussure and, in rather different terms, by Peirce. **Semiosis** is the generation of meaning on the basis of signification, and the **semiotic medium** is any material carrying a sequence of signs: at one level, voiced or instrumental sounds, print on paper, light recorded on film, paint and canvas, timber or stone; at another, the organisation of this material base in the form of pitch and tone, layout and syntax, mass and line, and so on.

Situation   In relation to the codes of text and genre, situation is a context which may exist in the form of actual speakers and a physical environment together with a structure of information that they carry, or may be virtual but still laden with information. The situation is at once a 'constellation of meanings' (Halliday) and a constraint on semiosis.

Speaking position   A position or role that I occupy when I speak or write and which is structured by the nature of the language I am using and by the structure of address, rather than by who I am as a person.

Speech act   The action performed by an utterance as part of a social interaction. The concept comes from Austin's recognition that commands, greetings, requests and so on do not assert propositional truths, and that the assertion of truths, the action with which philosophy is preoccupied, is only one of a number of acts performed by language.

Speech situation   The disposition of positions of speaking and any other relevant contextual circumstances which organises an act of speech or writing.

Structure of address   The organisation of relations between speaking positions in a particular situation.

Subject   Here, the relevant dimension of this word is the grammatical, which relates one part of the sentence to that which is predicated of it; the entity spoken of in the sentence.

Subject of utterance, subject of enunciation   I distinguish these two terms here as the self projected in discourse and the self who speaks; the former is a structural position constructed in language, the latter is the speaking self constructed in its occupation of that position.

Symbolic action   Any work of signification which effects changes in its environment.

System   Any set of relations between elements such that their meaning and/or their function is assigned only by virtue of those relations, and any change in an element alters all other elements. All systems are sufficiently closed to be coherent, and sufficiently open-ended to exchange information with other systems; the consequence of the latter property is that systems are always in a greater or lesser degree of transformation.

Taxonomy   Systematic classification.

Text, textuality   Any organisation of one or more utterances that is recognised by some receiver as a meaningful communication. The concept is not restricted to speech or writing: it can be applied to any medium of expression, or any combination of media. Although we usually speak of 'a' text as an actualised instance of discourse, an event in place and time, the more precise sense of the word refers as well to the organisation that underlies that instance. The concept of **textuality** refers to the fact of being a text and to the properties usually assigned to this organisation, characteristically properties of pattern and of the dynamic and open-ended transformation of meaning; Hanks (1989: 96) defines it as 'the quality of coherence or connectivity that characterises text'.

Thematic   Having to do with a recurrent and conventional set of ideas, arguments, or objects of discourse.

Topic, *topos*, *topoi*   Any recurrent organisation of textual content. A *topos* (pl. *topoi*) is a commonplace, something originally written in a commonplace book as part of a store of possible topics of conversation or writing.

Translation   The regular modification of the formal properties of a text in its transfer from one context to another.

Truth effects   Like 'reality effects', a term developed to explain in relative rather than absolute terms the kinds of truths elaborated in and by texts (of any kind).

Use value   The concept is half of a binary articulated in the writings of Marx, designating the inherent and specific value of things, grounded in their physical properties, and opposed to exchange value, the abstract value form that allows singular things to be equated with other singular and unlike things as though they were equivalent.

World   The 'real' world is the sum of everything that there is, including unreal things such as fictions, and possibly – depending who you believe – possible things. The concept of 'world' as I use it in this book is restricted to any coherent organisation of meaning or experience which works as a schematically reduced version of the 'real' world.

BIBLIOGRAPHY

Abrahams, Roger D. (1985) 'A Note on Neck-Riddles in the West Indies as They Comment on Emergent Genre Theory', *The Journal of American Folklore*, 98:387, 85–94.

Altman, Rick (1987) *The American Film Musical*, Bloomington: Indiana University Press.

—— (1999) *Film/Genre*, London: BFI.

Aristotle (1941) 'Poetics', trans. Ingram Bywater, in *The Basic Works of Aristotle*, ed. Richard McKeon, New York: Random House, 1454–87.

Armstrong, Nancy (1987) *Desire and Domestic Fiction: A Political History of the Novel*, New York: Oxford University Press.

Austen, Jane (1966 [1814]) *Mansfield Park*, ed. Tony Tanner, Harmondsworth: Penguin.

Austin, J.L. (1962) *How To Do Things With Words*, Oxford: The Clarendon Press.

Bakhtin, M.M. (1981) *The Dialogic Imagination*, trans. Caryl Emerson and Michael Holquist, Austin: University of Texas Press.

—— (1984) *Problems of Dostoevsky's Poetics*, ed. and trans. Caryl Emerson, Minneapolis: University of Minnesota Press.

—— (1986) *Speech Genres and Other Late Essays*, trans. Vern W. McGee, ed. Caryl Emerson and Michael Holquist, Austin: University of Texas Press.

Bakhtin, M.M./Medvedev, P.M. (1985) *The Formal Method in Literary Scholarship*, trans. Albert J. Wehrle, Cambridge, MA: Harvard University Press.

Bann, Stephen (2003) 'Questions of Genre in Early Nineteenth-Century French Painting', *New Literary History*, 34:3, 501–11.

Barthes, Roland (1990) *S/Z*, trans. Richard Miller, Oxford: Blackwell.

Bateson, Gregory (1973) *Steps to an Ecology of Mind: Collected Essays in Anthropology, Psychiatry, Evolution and Epistemology*, St Albans: Paladin.

Bauman, Richard and Briggs, Charles L. (1990) 'Poetics and Performance as Critical Perspectives on Language and Social Life', *Annual Review of Anthropology*, 19, 59–88.

Bauman, Richard and Sherzer, Joel, eds, (1974) *Explorations in the Ethnography of Speaking*, Cambridge: Cambridge University Press.

Beaujour, Michel (1980) 'Genus Universum', *Glyph*, 7, 15–31.

Beebee, Thomas O. (1994) *The Ideology of Genre: A Comparative Study of Generic Instability*, University Park, Pennsylvania: The Pennsylvania State University Press.

Behrens, Irene (1940) *Die Lehre von der Einteilung der Dichtkunst, vornehmlich vom 16. bis 19. Jahrhundert: Studien zur Geschichte der poetischen Gattungen*, Halle: Niemeyer.

Benjamin, Walter (1996) 'Goethe's Elective Affinities', trans. Stanley Corngold, in *Selected Writings, Vol. 1: 1913–1926*, eds Marcus Bullock and Michael W. Jennings, Cambridge, MA: Harvard University Press, 297–360.

Bennett, Tony (1990) *Outside Literature*, London: Routledge.

Bennett, Tony, Emmison, Michael and Frow, John (1999) *Accounting for Tastes: Australian Everyday Cultures*, Cambridge: Cambridge University Press.

Biguenet, John (1998) 'Double Takes: The Role of Allusion in Cinema', in Horton and McDougal, eds, 131–43.

Blanchot, Maurice (1959) *Le Livre à Venir*, Paris: Gallimard.

Bloomfield, Morton W. (1986) 'The Elegy and the Elegiac Mode', in Lewalski, ed., 147–57.

Bowker, Geoffrey C. and Star, Susan Leigh (1999) *Sorting Things Out: Classification and its Consequences*, Cambridge, MA: MIT Press.

Braudel, Fernand (1972 and 1973) *The Mediterranean and the Mediterranean World in the Age of Philip II*, trans. Siân Reynolds, 2 vols, London: Collins.

Briggs, Charles L. and Bauman, Richard (1992) 'Genre, Intertextuality, and Social Power', *Journal of Linguistic Anthropology*, 2:2, 131–72.

Brunetière, Ferdinand (1890) *L'Evolution des genres dans l'histoire de la littérature*, 2 vols, Paris: Hachette.

Caillois, Roger (1986) 'Riddles and Images', trans. Jeffrey Mehlman, *Yale French Studies*, 41, 148–58.

Campbell, Karlyn and Jamieson, Kathleen (1978) eds, *Form and Genre: Shaping Rhetorical Action*, Falls Church, Virginia: Speech Communication Association.

—— (1978) 'Form and Genre in Rhetorical Criticism: An Introduction', in Campbell and Jamieson, eds, 18–25.

Capgrave, John (1858) *The Chronicle of England*, London: Longman.

Certeau, Michel de (1986) *Heterologies: Discourse on the Other*, trans. Brian Massumi, Minneapolis: University of Minnesota Press.

Chambers, Ross (1984) *Story and Situation: Narrative Seduction and the Power of Fiction*, Minneapolis: University of Minnesota Press.

Christie, Frances (1993) 'Curriculum Genres: Planning for Effective Teaching', in Cope and Kalantzis, eds, 154–78.

Coe, Richard, Lingard, Lorelei and Teslenko, Tatiana, (2002) eds, *The Rhetoric and Ideology of Genre: Strategies for Stability and Change*, Creskill, NJ: Hampton Press.

—— (2002) 'Genre as Action, Strategy, and Différance: An Introduction', in Coe *et al.*, eds, 1–10.

Cohen, Ralph, ed., (1989) *The Future of Literary Theory*, New York: Routledge.

Colie, Rosalie (1973) *The Resources of Kind: Genre-Theory in the Renaissance*, Berkeley: University of California Press.

Cope, Bill and Kalantzis, Mary (1993) eds, *The Powers of Literacy: A Genre Approach to Teaching Writing*, London: The Falmer Press.

—— (1993) 'Introduction: How a Genre Approach to Literacy Can Transform the Way Writing is Taught', in Cope and Kalantzis, eds, 1–21.

Cortazar, Julio (1966) *Hopscotch*, trans. Gregory Rabassa, London: Collins.

Croce, Benedetto (2000) 'Criticism of the Theory of Artistic and Literary Kinds', in Duff, ed., 25–8.

Derrida, Jacques (1976) *Of Grammatology*, trans. Gayatri Chakravorty Spivak, Baltimore: Johns Hopkins University Press.

—— (1980) 'The Law of Genre', trans. Avital Ronell, *Glyph*, 7, 202–32.

Dorst, John D. (1983) 'Neck-riddle as a Dialogue of Genres: Applying Bakhtin's Genre Theory', *The Journal of American Folklore*, 96: 382, 413–33.

Draper, John W. (1967 [1929]) *The Funeral Elegy and the Rise of English Romanticism*, London: Frank Cass.

Dubrow, Heather (1982) *Genre*, London: Methuen.

Ducrot, Oswald and Todorov, Tzvetan (1981) *Encyclopedic Dictionary of the Sciences of Language*, trans. Catherine Porter, Oxford: Blackwell.

Duff, David (2000) ed., *Modern Genre Theory,* Harlow: Longman.

—— (2000) 'Introduction', in Duff, ed., 1–24.

Empson, William (1966 [1935]) *Some Versions of Pastoral*, Harmondsworth: Penguin.

Etiemble, René (1962) 'Histoire des genres et littérature comparée', *Acta Litteraria*, 5, 203–7.

Farrell, Joseph (2003) 'Classical Genre in Theory and Practice', *New Literary History*, 34:3, 383–408.

Ferrell, Robyn (2002) *Genres of Philosophy*, London: Ashgate.

Fishelov, David (1993) *Metaphors of Genre: The Role of Analogies in Genre Theory*, University Park, PA: The Pennsylvania State University Press.

Fletcher, Angus (1964) *Allegory: The Theory of a Symbolic Mode*, Ithaca: Cornell University Press.

Foucault, Michel (1989) *The Archaeology of Knowledge*, trans. A.M. Sheridan Smith, London: Routledge.

Fowler, Alastair (1982) *Kinds of Literature: An Introduction to the Theory of Genres and Modes*, Cambridge, MA: Harvard University Press.

Freadman, Anne (1986) 'Le Genre Humain (a Classification)', *Australian Journal of French Studies*, 23:3, 309–74.

—— (1988) 'Untitled: (On Genre)', *Cultural Studies*, 2:1, 67–99.

—— (2002) 'Uptake', in Coe *et al.*, eds, 39–53.

—— (2004) *The Machinery of Talk: Charles Peirce and the Sign Hypothesis*, Stanford: Stanford University Press.

Freedman, Aviva and Medway, Peter (1994) eds, *Genre and the New Rhetoric*, London: Taylor & Francis.

—— (1994) 'Locating Genre Studies: Antecedents and Prospects', in Freedman and Medway, eds, 1–20.

Freud, Sigmund (1960 [1905]) *Jokes and their Relation to the Unconscious*, trans. James Strachey, London: Routledge and Kegan Paul.

Frow, John (1986) *Marxism and Literary History*, Cambridge, MA: Harvard University Press.

Frye, Northrop (1963) 'Literature as Context: Milton's *Lycidas*', in *Fables of Identity: Studies in Poetic Mythology*, New York: Harcourt, Brace and World, 119–29.

—— (1967 [1957]) *Anatomy of Criticism*, New York: Atheneum.

—— (1976) *Spiritus Mundi*, Bloomington: Indiana University Press.

Gazdar, Gerald (1979) *Pragmatics: Implicature, Presupposition, and Logical Form*, New York: Academic Press.

Genette, Gérard (1992 [1979]) *The Architext: An Introduction*, trans. Jane E. Lewin, Berkeley: University of California Press.

—— (1997 [1987]) *Paratexts: Thresholds of Interpretation*, trans. Jane E. Lewin, Cambridge: Cambridge University Press.

Genette, Gérard and Todorov, Tzvetan, eds (1986) *Théorie des genres*, Paris: Ed. du Seuil.

Georges, Robert A. and Dundes, Alan (1963) 'Toward a Structural Definition of the Riddle', *The Journal of American Folklore*, 76:300, 111–18.

Giltrow, Janet (2002) 'Meta-Genre', in Coe *et al.*, eds, 187–205.

Goethe, Johann Wolfgang (1966 [1819]) 'Noten und Abhandlungen zum besseren Verständnis des West-östlichen Divans', in *Gedenkausgabe der Werke, Briefe und Gespräche*, vol. 3, third edition, Zurich: Artemis Verlag, 413–566.

—— (1971 [1809]) *Elective Affinities*, trans. R.J. Hollingdale, Harmondsworth: Penguin.

Goffman, Erving (1974) *Frame Analysis: An Essay on the Organisation of Experience*, New York: Harper and Row.

—— (1981) *Forms of Talk*, Oxford: Basil Blackwell.

Grice, Paul (1989) *Studies in the Way of Words*, Cambridge, MA: Harvard University Press.

Guérard, Albert (1940) *Preface to World Literature*, New York: Holt.

Guillén, Claudio (1971) 'On the Uses of Literary Genre', in *Literature as System: Essays Toward the Theory of Literary History*, Princeton: Princeton University Press, 107–34.

—— (1986) 'Notes Toward the Study of the Renaissance Letter', in Lewalski, ed., 70–101.

Haas, C. (1994) 'Learning to Read Biology: One Student's Rhetorical Development in College', *Written Communication*, 11, 43–84.

Halliday, M.A.K. (1978) *Language as Social Semiotic*, London: Edward Arnold.

Hamnett, Ian (1967) 'Ambiguity, Classification and Change: The Function of Riddles', *Man*, n.s., 2:3, 379–92.

Hanks, William F. (1989) 'Text and Textuality', *Annual Review of Anthropology*, 18, 95–127.

—— (1996) *Language and Communicative Practices*, Boulder: Westview Press.

—— (2000) *Intertexts: Writings on Language, Utterance, and Context*, Lanham: Rowman and Littlefield.

Haring, Lee (1974) 'On Knowing the Answer', *The Journal of American Folklore*, 87:345, 197–207.

—— (1985) 'Malagasy Riddling', *The Journal of American Folklore,* 98:388, 163–90.

Hegel, G.W.F. (1975) *Aesthetics: Lectures on Fine Art*, trans. T.M. Knox, Oxford: Clarendon Press.

Hempfer, Klaus N. (1973) *Gattungstheorie*, Munich: Wilhelm Fink.

Hernardi, Paul (1972) *Beyond Genre*, Ithaca: Cornell University Press.

Hirsch, E.D., Jr. (1967) *Validity in Interpretation*, New Haven: Yale University Press.

Holquist, Michael (1981) 'Introduction' in Bakhtin (1981), xv–xxxiv.

Horton, Andrew and McDougal, Stuart Y., eds (1998) *Play It Again, Sam: Retakes on Remakes*, Berkeley: University of California Press.

Hymes, Dell (1974) 'Ways of Speaking', in Bauman and Sherzer, eds, 433–51.

Imbrie, Ann E. (1986) 'Defining Nonfiction Genres', in Lewalski, ed., 45–69.

Jamieson, Kathleen and Campbell, Karlyn (1982) 'Rhetorical Hybrids: Fusions of Generic Elements', *Quarterly Journal of Speech*, 68, 146–57.

Jauss, H.R. (1982) 'Theory of Genres and Medieval Literature', in *Toward an Aesthetic of Reception*, trans. Timothy Bahti, Minneapolis: University of Minnesota Press, 76–109.

Jenny, Laurent (1982) 'The Strategy of Form', in Todorov, ed. (1982), 34–63.

Johns, Ann M. (1997) *Text, Role, and Context: Developing Academic Literacies*, Cambridge: Cambridge University Press.

Jolles, André (1968) *Einfache Formen: Legende, Sage, Mythe, Rätsel, Spruch, Kasus, Memorabile, Märchen, Witz*, Tübingen: Niemeyer.

Joyce, James (1960 [1916]) *A Portrait of the Artist as a Young Man*, Harmondsworth: Penguin.

Kallen, Jeffrey L. and Eastman, Carol M. (1979) ' "I went to Mombasa, There I Met an Old Woman": Structure and Meaning in Swahili Riddles', *The Journal of American Folklore*, 92:366, 418–44.

Keenan, Thomas (1997) *Fables of Responsibility: Aberrations and Predicaments in Ethics and Politics*, Stanford: Stanford University Press.

Kermode, Frank (1966) *The Sense of an Ending: Studies in the Theory of Fiction*, Oxford: Oxford University Press.

Kintsch, Walter (1998) *Comprehension: A Paradigm for Cognition*, Cambridge: Cambridge University Press.

Kress, Gunther (1993) 'Genre as Social Process', in Cope and Kalantzis, eds, 22–37.

Kress, Gunther and Threadgold, Terry (1988) 'Towards a Social Theory of Genre', *Southern Review*, 21:3, 215–43.

Laclos, Choderlos de (1961 [1782]) *Les Liaisons dangéreuses*, trans. P.W.K. Stone, Harmondsworth: Penguin.

Lacoue-Labarthe, Philippe and Nancy, Jean-Luc (1988) *The Literary Absolute: The Theory of Literature in German Romanticism*, trans. Philip Barnard and Cheryl Lester, Albany: SUNY Press.

Lakoff, George (1987) *Women, Fire, and Dangerous Things: What Categories Reveal About the Mind*, Chicago: University of Chicago Press.

Lecercle, Jean-Jacques (1999) *Interpretation as Pragmatics*, London: Macmillan.

Levinson, Stephen C. (1983) *Pragmatics*, Cambridge: Cambridge University Press.

Lewalski, Barbara Kiefer (1986) ed., *Renaissance Genres: Essays on Theory, History, and Interpretation*, Cambridge, MA: Harvard University Press.

—— (1986) 'Introduction: Issues and Approaches', in Lewalski, ed., 1–12.

Lewis, David (1986) *On the Plurality of Worlds*, Oxford: Basil Blackwell.

Lukács, Georg (1969) *Probleme der Ästhetik, Werke*, vol. 10, Neuwied: Luchterhand.

—— (1971) *The Theory of the Novel: A Historico-Philosophical Essay on the Forms of Great Epic Literature,* trans. Anna Bostock, Cambridge, MA: MIT Press.

McCarthy, Michael and Carter, Ronald (1994) *Language as Discourse: Perspectives for Language Teaching*, London: Longman.

McKeon, Michael (1987) *The Origins of the English Novel 1600–1740*, Baltimore: Johns Hopkins University Press.

MacLachlan, Gale and Reid, Ian (1994) *Framing and Interpretation*, Melbourne: Melbourne University Press.

Malik, Rachel (2002) *Fixing Meaning: Intertextuality, Inferencing and Genre in Interpretation*, PhD thesis, Middlesex University.

Malinowski, Bronislaw (1935) *Coral Gardens and their Magic: A Study of the Methods of Tilling the Soil and of Agricultural Rites in the Trobriand Islands*, 2 vols, London: Allen and Unwin.

Mandler, Jean Matter (1984) *Stories, Scripts, and Scenes: Aspects of Schema Theory*, Hillsdale, NJ: Erlbaum.

Miller, Carolyn R. (1994a) 'Genre as Social Action', in Freedman and Medway, eds, 23–42.

—— (1994b) 'Rhetorical Community: The Cultural Basis of Genre', in Freedman and Medway, eds, 67–78.

Miller, J. Hillis (1992) *Ariadne's Thread: Story Lines*, New Haven: Yale University Press.

Miller, Paul Allen (2004) *Subjecting Verses: Latin Love Elegy and the Emergence of the Real*, Princeton: Princeton University Press.

Miner, Earl (1986) 'Some Issues of Literary "Species, or Distinct Kind" ', in Lewalski, ed, 15–44.

Muir, Bernard J., ed. (2000) *The Exeter Anthology of Old English Poetry*, 2 vols, Exeter: University of Exeter Press.

Neale, Steve (2000) *Genre and Hollywood*, London: Routledge.

O'Hara, Frank (1974) *The Selected Poems of Frank O'Hara*, ed. Donald Allen, New York: Vintage Books.

Opie, Iona and Opie, Peter, eds (1952) *The Oxford Dictionary of Nursery Rhymes*, Oxford: Clarendon Press.

Paltridge, Brian (1997) *Genre, Frames and Writing in Research Settings*, Amsterdam and Philadelphia: John Benjamins.

Pêcheux, Michel (1975) *Les Vérités de la Palice*, Paris: Maspéro.

Perpicello, W.J. and Green, Thomas A. (1984) *The Language of Riddles: New Perspectives*, Columbus: Ohio University Press.

Phillips, Mark Salber (2003) 'Histories, Micro- and Literary: Problems of Genre and Distance', *New Literary History*, 34:2, 211–29.

Pigman, G.W. (1985) *Grief and English Renaissance Elegy*, Cambridge: Cambridge University Press.

Plato (1961) 'The Republic', trans. Paul Shorey, in *The Collected Dialogues of Plato*, Princeton: Princeton University Press, 576–844.

Potts, Abbie Findlay (1967) *The Elegiac Mode: Poetic Form in Wordsworth and Other Elegists*, Ithaca: Cornell University Press.

Ramsdell, Kristin (1999) *Romance Fiction: A Guide to the Genre*, Englewood, Colo.: Libraries Unlimited.

Reid, Ian (1984) *The Making of Literature: Texts, Contexts and Classroom Practices*, Np: Australian Association for the Teaching of English.

Rosmarin, Adena (1985) *The Power of Genre*, Minneapolis: University of Minnesota Press.

Roubaud, Jacques (1995 [1991]) *The Plurality of Worlds of Lewis*, trans. Rosmarie Waldrop, Normal, IL: Dalkey Archive Press.

Sacks, Peter (1985) *The English Elegy: Studies in the Genre from Spenser to Yeats*, Baltimore: Johns Hopkins University Press.

Schaeffer, Jean-Marie (1986) 'Du texte au genre', in Genette and Todorov, eds, 179–205.

—— (1989) 'Literary Genres and Textual Genericity', trans. Alice Otis, in Cohen, ed., 67–87.

Schlegel, Friedrich (1957) *Literary Notebooks 1797–1801*, ed. Hans Eichner, London: The Athlone Press.

Schryer, Catherine F. (1994) 'The Lab versus the Clinic: Sites of Competing Genres', in Freedman and Medway, eds, 105–24.

Schutz, Alfred (1970) *On Phenomenology and Social Relations: Selected Writings*, Chicago: University of Chicago Press.

Scott, Charles T. (1965) *Persian and Arabic Riddles: A Language-Centred Approach to Genre Definition*, Bloomington: Indiana Research Centre in Anthropology, Folklore and Linguistics.

Seitel, Peter (2003) 'Theorising Genres – Interpreting Works', *New Literary History*, 34:2, 275–97.

Sherzer, Joel (1983) *Kuna Ways of Speaking*, Austin: University of Texas Press.

Silverstein, Michael and Urban, Greg (1996) eds, *Natural Histories of Discourse*, Chicago: University of Chicago Press.

—— (1996) 'The Natural History of Discourse', in Silverstein and Urban, eds, 1–17.

Sperber, Dan and Wilson, Deirdre (1986) *Relevance: Communication and Cognition*, Cambridge, MA: Harvard University Press.

Staiger, Emil (1991) *Basic Concepts of Poetics*, trans. Janette C. Hudson and Luanne T. Frank, University Park: Pennsylvania State University Press.

Swales, John M. (1990) *Genre Analysis: English in Academic and Research Settings*, Cambridge: Cambridge University Press.

Tacitus, Cornelius (1964) *The Annals and the Histories*, trans. A.J. Church and W.J. Brodribb, New York: Washington Square Press.

Tanner, Tony (1979) *Adultery in the Novel: Contract and Transgression*, Baltimore: Johns Hopkins University Press.

Taylor, Archer (1951) *English Riddles from Oral Tradition*, Berkeley: University of California Press.

—— (1976 [1948]) *The Literary Riddle Before 1600*, Westport, CT: Greenwood Press.

Threadgold, Terry (1988) 'The Genre Debate', *Southern Review*, 21:3, 315–30.

—— (1989) 'Talking About Genre: Ideologies and Incompatible Discourses', *Cultural Studies*, 3:1, 101–27.

Tiffany, Daniel (2001) 'Lyric Substance: On Riddles, Materialism, and Poetic Obscurity', *Critical Inquiry*, 28:1, 72–98.

Todorov, Tzvetan (1975) *The Fantastic*, trans. Richard Howard, Ithaca: Cornell University Press.

—— (1978) 'La Devinette', in Todorov, *Les Genres du discours*, Paris: Ed. du Seuil, 223–45.

—— (1982) ed., *French Literary Theory Today*, trans. R. Carter, Cambridge: Cambridge University Press.

—— (1990) *Genres in Discourse*, trans. Catherine Porter, Cambridge: Cambridge University Press.

Tynianov, Yuri (2003) 'The Ode as an Oratorical Genre', trans. Ann
    Shukman, *New Literary History*, 34:3, 565–96.
Viëtor, Karl (1986) 'L'histoire des genres littéraires', in Genette and
    Todorov, eds, 9–35.
Volosinov, V.N. (1973) *Marxism and the Philosophy of Language*, trans.
    Ladislav Matejka and I.R. Titunik, London: Seminar Press.
Welsh, Andrew (1978) *Roots of Lyric: Primitive Poetry and Modern Poetics*,
    Princeton: Princeton University Press.
Wittgenstein, Ludwig (1968 [1953]) *Philosophical Investigations*, trans.
    G.E.M. Anscombe, Oxford: Basil Blackwell.

FILMS

A Chorus Line (1985), Dir. Richard Attenborough
Forty-Second Street (1933), Dir. Lloyd Bacon)
Gone With the Wind (1939), Dir. Victor Fleming
Home Alone (1990), Dir. Chris Columbus
Nosferatu, eine Symphonie des Grauens (1921), Dir. F.W. Murnau
Nosferatu: Phantom der Nacht (1979), Dir. Werner Herzog
Out of Africa (1985), Dir. Sydney Pollack
Pretty Woman (1990), Dir. Garry Marshall
Showboat (1936), Dir. James Whale
Showboat (1951), Dir. George Sidney
The Player (1992), Dir. Robert Altman

INDEX

A Chorus Line 49
Abrahams, Roger 38
Addison, Joseph 150
Aeschylus 62
Altman, Rick 52–53, 102, 104, 114, 137–139
Altman, Robert *The Player* 138
archigenres 64
Aristophanes 151
Aristotle 3, 25, 26, 53, 55–57, 59, 64, 65, 93, 150
Armstrong, Nancy 136–137
Auden, W.H. 133
Austen, Jane *Emma* 65; *Mansfield Park* 46–47, 119
Austin, John 151, 152

Bakhtin, Mikhail 3, 18, 29, 30, 42, 43, 44, 45, 57, 58, 67, 104, 136, 145, 147
Bann, Stephen 125
Barthes, Roland 58
Bateson, Gregory 46
Batteux, Charles 150
Bauman, Richard 45, 48
Beaujour, Michel 27, 28
Beebee, Thomas 25, 52, 101, 134
Behrens, Irene 59
Benjamin, Walter 117, 121, 122
Bennett, Tony 137, 139
Biguenet, John 49
Blair, Robert *The Grave* 132
Blake, William 133
Blanchot, Maurice 26, 27
Bloomfield, Morton 132, 134
Boileau, Nicolas 59, 150
Bovet, Ernest 60
Bowker, Geoffrey 12, 13, 51, 53–55
Braudel, Fernand 97–99
Briggs, Charles 45, 48

Browning, Robert 62
Brunetière, Ferdinand 52–53
Byron, George Gordon 62; *Childe Harold* 67; *Don Juan* 67

Caillois, Roger 35
Campbell, Karlyn 14
Capgrave, John 95
Carroll, Lewis 66
Carter, Ronald 143
ceremony 16, 17, 24
Certeau, Michel de 93–94, 98
Cervantes, Miguel de 59
Chambers, Ross 115
Christie, Frances 140
Cicero 150
citation 3, 26, 28, 42, 44, 45, 48, 145
classification 2, 3, 12, 13, 25, 51–55, 59, 103
Coe, Richard 14
Colie, Rosalie 18, 19, 92–93
contract 3, 52, 104, 116
Cope, Bill 141–142
Cortazar, Julio *Hopscotch* 122
counterfactuals 89, 91
Croce, Benedetto 27
cue 4, 84, 104, 105, 109–114, 115

Darwin, Charles 51
decorum 57, 75, 76, 145
Deleuze, Gilles 150, 152
Derrida, Jacques 3, 25, 26, 28, 42, 152
dialogue, dialogic 34, 41, 42, 43, 57, 145
Dickens, Charles 66; *A Tale of Two Cities* 62; *Bleak House* 131; *David Copperfield* 131
Diomedes 59
discourse 10, 12, 17, 18, 24, 42, 43, 44, 48, 75, 76, 77, 83, 87, 106, 124, 145–146

discourse community 7
discursive formation 77
discursive practice 35
Dorst, John 38–9, 40
Dostoevsky, Fyodor 136; *Crime and Punishment* 131
Draper, John 132
Dryden, John 59, 150
Dubrow, Heather 104
Ducrot, Oswald 69
Duff, David 60
Dundes, Alan 32

Eastman, Carol 35
Eichenbaum, Boris 152
Empson, William 66
Epic of Gilgamesh 54
Etiemble, René 134
Exeter Book 37

family, family resemblance 3, 52, 54, 70
Farrell, Joseph 133–134
Ferrell, Robyn 87, 90
Fishelov, David 52, 53
Fletcher, Angus 66
formal features, formal organisation, formal structure 4, 8, 9, 11, 15, 72, 74, 76, 94, 110, 114, 135, 141, 147
Forty-Second Street 49
Foucault, Michel 17, 18, 87, 99, 146, 149
Fowler, Alastair 3, 54, 65, 66, 133
frame, framework 3, 9, 10, 11, 17, 18, 19, 34, 46, 72, 73, 74, 79, 80, 81, 83, 85, 92, 93, 101, 102, 103–109, 112, 114, 143, 147
Freadman, Anne 16, 17, 24, 26, 88
Freud, Sigmund 33, 151
Frow, John 68, 107, 139
Frye, Northrop 19, 20, 35, 64, 66

Gallus 131
Gay, John 66

Gazdar, Gerald 77
Genesis 54
Genette, Gérard 57, 62, 64, 65, 105–106, 109
Genreflecting 128–130
genres and sub-genres:
    of film and television: art movie 125, biopic 138, documentary 17, 72–73, drama 113, fairy-tale musical 114, feature film 72, *film noir* 66, 139, folk musical 114, heist movie 1, home movie 17, horror movie 66, musical 51, 103, 104, 111–114, 138, 'old house' movie 66, psychological drama 102, putting-on-a-show musical 112, 114, sitcom 65, 86, 104, 115, teen movie 125, telemovie 102, television advertisement 125, 131, television programme 125, thriller 51, 65, Western 1, 23, 138, 'woman's film' 139
    of painting: *genre historique* 125, genre painting 1, *genre secondaire* 125
    of music: ball-bouncing song 111, ballad 59, 60, 75, 110, flute song 134, lullaby 110, military march 75, milonga 125, nocturne 75, raga 75, skipping song 110, tango 125, techno 75
    of architecture: hut 30, cottage 30, fortified keep 30, store room 30, cell 30, temple 30
    of writing: allegory 60, annal 95–96, anniversary 132, autobiographical memoir 136, bill of lading 93, biography 44, bureaucratic document 84, chanson de geste 71, chronicle 95–96, comedy 51, 56, 57, 58, 59, confession 44, 90, detective fiction 1, 31,36, 65, 66, dialogue 90, diary 44, didactic 58, digest 15, drama 30, 45, 58, 59, 60, 62, 63, dream-narrative 111, eclogue 66,

elegy 5, 19, 21, 58, 59, 60, 65, 77, 131–134, 137, elegy of lamentation 133, email 100, emblem 31, epic 45, 54, 57, 58, 59, 62, 63, 125, 135, epicede 132, epigram 59, 131, epistle 60, epitaph 108–109, 132, essay 63, 140, fable 60, 111, 115, fabliau 71, feuilleton 63, funeral elegy 132, 133, funeral ode 132, genealogy 94, georgic 66, gothic romance 66, 84, government edict 93, haiku 77, headline 7, 14, 80, 83, 84, historical novel 65, iambic 58, idyll 59, 60, introductory guide 2, journal 122, letter 44, 46–48, 64, 66, 77, 93, 100, 136, love elegy 133, love poem 131, lyric 20, 56, 58, 59, 62, 63, 131, madrigal 59, melodrama 66, Metaphysical lyric 31, *monogotari* 134, multiple-choice exam 140, news story 125, newspaper editorial 125, newspaper report 63, 72, novel 23, 25, 27, 29, 30, 43, 45, 60, 63, 65, 114, 120–123, 134–137, *novela* 134, novella 120–123, novel of manners 65, novel of ideas 65, ode 59, 60, 125, *pantun* 31, opinion column 125, parable 108, parody 60, pastoral 19, 58, picaresque novel 65, 86, polemical satire 63, political satire 131, puzzle 63, report 141, research essay 141, *roman* 134, romance 60,129, 134, 140, rondeau 59, satire 58,59, 60, science fiction 1, song 59, sonnet 59, 76, 86, street poster 73, technical paper 90, tragedy 8, 51, 56, 57, 58, 59, tragicomedy 59, travel notes 44, *tristan* 71, *troja* 71, vampire novel 66, vaudeville 59, weblog 77

oral genres: aphorism 77, catechism questions 32, chant 29, charm 29, 35, children's story 23, classroom discussion 140, conversation 79, counting-out rhyme 110, curse 86, debate 140, dithyramb 56, 57, 59, 146, eulogy 24, everyday talk 68, eyewitness testimony 95, 'faggot' joke 115, formal address 63, funeral sermon 132, *ikar* 45, imprecation 22, joke 51, *koan* 32, military command 29, neck riddle 32, 35, 38–39, nursery rhyme 110–111, oedipal riddle 35, prayer 24, 29, 133, prophetic riddle 40, proverb 49, 63, 110, quiz question 32, reminiscence 95, riddle 3, 29- 40, 51, 68, 73–74, 110, 111, self-talk 22, sermon 23, 24, shaggy-dog story 29, story 93, street cry 110, technical talk 68

legal genres: case 8, cross-examination 16, deposition 16, legal document 114, oath-taking 16, pronouncement of sentence 16, summing-up 16

genrification 137–139
Georges, Robert 32
Giltrow, Janet 12
Goethe, Johann Wolfgang 60, 62, 68, 69; *Elective Affinities* 116- 123
Goffman, Erving 21, 22, 23, 34, 35–36, 42, 46, 106, 148
Gone with the Wind 113
Gongóra, Luis de 63
Gray, Thomas *Elegy Written in a Country Churchyard* 132
Green, Thomas 32
Greene, Graham *Stamboul Train: An Entertainment* 105
Grice, Paul 77–80, 148
Guérard, Albert 62, 65
Guillén, Claudio 64, 66

Haas, C. 140
Halliday, Michael 16, 152
Hamnett, Ian 33
Hanks, William 18, 97, 154

Haring, Lee 31, 36
Hegel, G.W.F. 60, 135
Heine, Heinrich 67
Hernardi, Paul 60, 63
Herzog, Werner Nosferatu: Phantom
    der Nacht, 49
Hesiod 58
heteroglossia 44, 136, 147
Hirsch, E.D. 101–102
historicism 97
Hölderlin, Friedrich 63
Holquist, Michael 66–67
Home Alone 49
Homer 55, 57; Iliad 54, 62; Odyssey 54
Horace 150
horizon of expectation 69–71, 147
Hugo, Victor Cromwell 61
Husserl 147
Hymes, Dell 23

Ibsen, Henrik 67
iconography 75, 147
Imbrie, Ann 73
imitation (mimesis) 55, 57, 63
implication, implicature 9, 77–83, 148
inference 79, 80–84, 101
institution, institutionalisation 52, 69,
    102–103, 128, 130, 137, 139, 140,
    148
intertextuality 3, 45, 48, 49, 114, 136,
    142, 148

Jakobson, Roman 152
James, Henry 58; The Golden Bowl
    121–122
Jamieson, Kathleen 14
Jauss, H.R. 28, 70–71, 76, 147
Jenny, Laurent 49
Johns, Ann 140
Johnson, Samuel 150
Jolles, André 3, 29, 30
Jonson, Ben On my first Daughter
    108–109
Joyce, James 61, 63

Kafka, Franz A Country Doctor 111; The
    Trial 131
Kalantzis, Mary 141–142
Kallen, Jeffrey 35
Keenan, Thomas 27
Kermode, Frank 148
keying 46, 148
Kintsch, Walter 85
knowledge nets 85
Kress, Gunther 143–144

Laclos, Choderlos de 48
Lacoue-Labarthe, Philippe 27
Lakoff, George 13
language game 31, 149
Lecercle, Jean-Jacques 84
Lejeune, Philippe 106
Levinson, Stephen 77–78
Lewalski, Barbara 66
Lewis, David 87–91
Linnaeus, Carl 51
Lucretius 58
Lukács, Georg 63, 134–136

McCarthy, Michael 143
McKeon, Michael 136
MacLachlan, Gale 107–109
Malik, Rachel 80
Malinowski, Bronislaw 16
Mallarmé, Stephane 63
Mandler, Jean Matter 84
Marx, Karl 155
Medvedev, P.M. 18
Menander 151
metaphors of genre 52–54
Miller, Carolyn 14, 46, 115, 144
Miller, Hillis 122
Miller, Paul Allen 131
Milton, John 59; Lycidas 19–21, 133
Miner, Earl 54
Minturno, Antonio Sebastiano 59
modal realism 88
modality 75, 90, 150
mode 4, 63–67, 77

modes: allegorical 66, comic 65, 66, didactic 66, dramatic 60, 61, 62, 65, 121, elegiac 65, 66, 132–134, epic 60, 61, 62, 65, encyclopaedic 66, epigrammatic 66, epistolary 66, fantastic 65, 66, gothic 65, 66, heroic 66, lyrical 60, 61, 62, 65, 66, melodramatic 66, novel as mode 67, pastoral 65, 66, romance 65, 66, satiric 65, 66, tragic 65, 66
Molière 62
morphology 53
Muir, Bernard 37
multiplicity 26, 28, 29, 99, 102, 150
Murnau, F.W. *Nosferatu: Eine Symphonie des Grauens* 49

Nancy, Jean-Luc 27
narration, narrative 55, 56, 57, 58, 59, 63, 67, 74, 93–99, 111, 113, 115–116, 121, 122, 135
natural forms 3, 60–64, 69
Neale, Steve 103
neo-classicism 52, 125, 145, 150
Nunn, Trevor 102
O'Hara, Frank *For James Dean* 132–133; *To the Film Industry in Crisis* 133
ontological domain 19
Opie, Iona and Peter 111
Ossian 131
Ovid 131

paideia 89
Paltridge, Brian 54
paratext 105–106
period 99
Perpicello, W.J. 32
Petersen, Julius 62
Phillips, Mark Salber 93
Pigman, G.W. 132
Pindar 146
Plato 3, 55–58, 59, 63, 64, 65, 88
Plautus 151
Poe, Edgar Allan 66

poetics 4, 58, 68, 70, 71, 151
position of enunciation 44, 63, 74, 146
Potts, Abbie Findlay 131
Pound, Ezra 29
pragmatics 64, 77
predicate 31, 32, 33, 34, 36, 40, 151
presentational modes 11, 57–59, 64, 65
presupposition 77, 81, 93
process pedagogy 141–142, 152
Propertius 77, 131
Propp, Vladimir 69
prototype 51, 54, 152
Prynne, J.H. 63

Quintilian 58, 150

radical of presentation 64, 66, 67
Ramsdell, Kristin 129
Rapin, René 59, 150
regime of reading 139–140
register 16, 143
Reid, Ian 107–109, 142–143
relevance 79, 82, 85
remake 49–50, 138
repetition 26, 48, 49
reported speech 3, 43, 45
resistance to genre 26, 27, 28
rhetorical authority 15
rhetorical structure, rhetorical function 4, 9, 11, 74, 76
Roman de Renart 70
Rosmarin, Adena 102, 109
Roubaud, Jacques 91–92
Russian Formalists 68, 130, 152

Sacks, Peter 134
Scaliger, Julius Caesar 133
Schaeffer, Jean-Marie 24, 53
schema 83–86, 102
Schlegel, Friedrich 27, 60; and August 27
Schryer, Catherine 28
Schutz, Alfred 87
Scott, Charles 36
secret 40

Seitel, Peter 86
semiosis 19, 101, 153
semiotic medium 57, 64, 67, 72, 73, 153
setting 9, 11, 14, 15, 16, 17, 73
Shakespeare, William 131; *Henry IV,
Part I* 105; *King Lear* 39; *Macbeth*
39–40, 45, 102; *The Tempest* 62
Shelley, Percy Bysshe 19, 20, 62
Sherzer, Joel 45
shops 126–128
Showboat (1951)103, 111–114
Showboat (1936) 113
Sidney, Philip 59, 66
simple forms 3, 17, 29–50, 94–95
situation 13, 15, 46, 107, 153
situation of address, situation of
utterance 9, 12, 74, 76
Socrates 55–57, 58, 62, 63, 90
speaking position 9, 108, 152
species 3, 52, 53, 56, 64
speech act 3, 52, 77
speech situation 41, 42, 47, 75, 82, 83,
115, 152
Sperber, Dan 80, 82
Staiger, Emil 62
Star, Susan Leigh 12, 13, 51, 53–55
structure of address, structure of
enunciation 9, 18, 36, 66, 73, 77, 152
sub-genre 65, 67, 114
subject of enunciation 42, 152
subject of utterance 42, 152
symbolic action 2, 10, 13, 152

Tacitus 96–97, 99
Tanner, Tony 119–120

taxonomy 3, 11, 13, 25, 26, 51–55, 143,
154
Taylor, Archer 31, 35, 36, 37, 38
Terence 151
thematic structure, thematic content 4,
9, 11, 64, 72, 75–76, 155
There was a Man of Double Deed
110–111
Theocritus 19, 58
Threadgold, Terry 143
Tibullus 77, 131
Tiffany, Daniel 37
Todorov, Tzvetan 34, 68, 69–71, 124
Tomashevsky, Boris 152
topos, topoi 9, 36, 73, 75, 90, 147, 155
translation 16, 28, 46, 155
Tynianov, Yuri 130, 152

Vergil 19; *Aeneid* 53
Viëtor, Karl 60
Volosinov, V.N. 29, 30, 43, 46, 48
Voltaire, François-Marie Arouet de 150

Watt, Ian 136
Welsh, Andrew 29
White, Hayden 97
Whitman, Walt 20, 21
Wilson, Deirdre 80, 82
Wittgenstein, Ludwig 54, 149
Wordsworth, William 20
world 4, 7, 18, 73, 74, 76, 85–87, 88–92,
98, 103, 155

Yeats, W.B. 133
Young, Edward *Night Thoughts* 132

Related titles from Routledge

Adaptation & Appropriation
Julie Sanders

the NEW CRITICAL IDIOM

From the apparently simple adaptation of a text into film, theatre or a new literary work, to the more complex appropriation of style or meaning, it is arguable that all texts are somehow connected to a network of existing texts and art forms.

Adaptation and Appropriation explores:

- multiple definitions and practices of adaptation and appropriation
- the cultural and aesthetic politics behind the impulse to adapt
- diverse ways in which contemporary literature and film adapt, revise and reimagine other works of art
- the impact on adaptation and appropriation of theoretical movements, including structuralism, post-structuralism, post-colonialism, postmodernism, feminism and gender studies
- the appropriation across time and across cultures of specific canonical texts, but also of literary archetypes such as myth or fairy tale.

Ranging across genres and harnessing concepts from fields as diverse as musicology and the natural sciences, this volume brings clarity to the complex debates around adaptation and appropriation, offering a much-needed resource for those studying literature, film or culture.

Hb: 0-415-31171-3
Pb: 0-415-31172-1

Available at all good bookshops
For ordering and further information please visit:
www.routledge.com

Related titles from Routledge

Intertextuality
Graham Allen

the NEW CRITICAL IDIOM

'NO TEXT HAS MEANING ALONE'
'ALL TEXTS HAVE MEANING IN RELATION TO OTHER TEXTS'

Graham Allen's Intertextuality follows all the major moves in the term's history, and clearly explores how intertextuality is employed in:

- Structuralism
- Post-structuralism
- Deconstruction
- Postcolonialism
- Marxism
- Feminism
- Psychoanalytic theory

With a wealth of illuminating examples from literary and cultural texts, including special examination of the World Wide Web, this book will prove invaluable for any student of literature and culture.

Hb: 0-415-17474-0
Pb: 0-415-17475-9

Available at all good bookshops
For ordering and further information please visit:
www.routledge.com

Related titles from Routledge

The Singularity of Literature
Derek Attridge

'Wonderfully original and challenging.'
J. Hillis Miller

Literature and the literary have proved singularly resistant to definition. Derek Attridge argues that such resistance represents not a dead end, but a crucial starting point from which to explore anew the power and practices of Western art.

In this lively, original volume, the author:

- Considers the implications of regarding the literary work as an innovative cultural event
- Provides a rich new vocabulary for discussions of literature, rethinking such terms as invention, singularity, otherness, alterity, performance and form
- Argues the ethical importance of the literary institution to a culture
- Demonstrates how a new understanding of the literary might be put to work in a "responsible", creative mode of reading

The Singularity of Literature is not only a major contribution to the theory of literature, but also a celebration of the extraordinary pleasure of the literary, for reader, writer, student or critic.

Hb: 0-415-33592-2
Pb: 0-415-33593-0

Available at all good bookshops
For ordering and further information please visit:
www.routledge.com

Related titles from Routledge

Genre and Hollywood
Steve Neale

Genre and Hollywood provides a comprehensive introduction to the study of genre. In this important new book, Steve Neale discusses all the major concepts, theories and accounts of Hollywood and genre, as well as the key genres which theorists have written about, from horror to the Western. He also puts forward new arguments about the importance of genre in understanding Hollywood cinema.

Neale takes issue with much genre criticism and genre theory, which has provided only a partial and misleading account of Hollywood's output. He calls for broader and more flexible conceptions of genre and genres, for more attention to be paid to the discourses and practices of Hollywood itself, for the nature and range of Hollywood's films to be looked at in more detail, and for any assessment of the social and cultural significance of Hollywood's genres to take account of industrial factors.

In detailed, revisionist accounts of two major genres - film noir and melodrama - Neale argues that genre remains an important and productive means of thinking about both New and old Hollywood, its history, its audiences and its films.

Hb: 0-415-02605-9
Pb: 0-415-02606-7

Available at all good bookshops
For ordering and further information please visit:
www.routledge.com